Commu

Faith

By the same author

Torah Studies

Tradition and Transition
(*editor*)

Tradition in an Untraditional Age

Arguments For The Sake Of Heaven

Orthodoxy Confronts Modernity
(*editor*)

The Persistence of Faith

Crisis and Covenant

One People?

Will We Have Jewish Grandchildren?

Faith in the Future

COMMUNITY OF FAITH

Jonathan Sacks

PETER HALBAN
LONDON

FIRST PUBLISHED IN GREAT BRITAIN BY
PETER HALBAN PUBLISHERS LTD
42 South Molton Street
London W1Y 1HB
1995

British Library Cataloguing in Publication Data

A catalogue record for this book is available from the British Library.

ISBN 1 870015 59 2

Typeset by Computape (Pickering) Ltd, North Yorkshire
Printed in Great Britain by
WBC Print, Bridgend

Contents

Preface

This book is my tribute to the United Synagogue on its 125th anniversary, in return for the many delights it has given me and the thousands of others who have been its members. In it I describe not its outward history but its spiritual foundations. Pascal once said, 'The heart has its reasons which reason does not know.' The same is often true of institutions. They have a dynamic of their own, an inner pulse and power, rarely formally articulated, but which needs to be understood if they are to be renewed. My subject is the synagogue as a living embodiment of the Jewish concept of community, in particular as it developed in Anglo-Jewry.

I have written it as a way of expressing my thanks to the many communities I have come to know since becoming Chief Rabbi four years ago. In my travels throughout Anglo-Jewry and the Commonwealth I have been moved, time and again, by their vigour, energy and warmth. This is due not only to their leaders, rabbinic and lay, whose dedication to the task of sustaining synagogue life is often tireless and sometimes thankless. It is also the achievement of countless men, women and young people who by quiet acts of kindness or hospitality give Jewish life its humanity and grace. In the words of one of our prayers, I offer thanks to 'those who unite to form synagogues for prayer, and those who come there to pray; those who provide lamps for lighting, wine for *kiddush* and *havdalah*, food for wayfarers and charity for the poor, and all who faithfully occupy themselves with the needs of the community'.

Special mention is owed to the Honorary Officers of the United Synagogue, Anthony Ansell, Anthony Cowen,

Maurice De Vries, Leslie Elstein, Stephen Forman, Alan Kennard and Elkan Levy, and its Chief Executive, Jonathan Lew. As I argue in this book, the heritage of which they are the custodians is rare in the contemporary Jewish world, and they have guarded it with dedication. I have had the privilege of working with two distinguished Presidents. Sidney Frosh, who led the United Synagogue when I came into office, is one of Anglo-Jewry's most beloved figures. It was with immense sadness that, as I was preparing this work, we mourned the loss of his beloved wife Ruth whose kindness we will long remember. Seymour Saideman, its current President, has steered it boldly through difficult times and hard decisions, taking it from financial crisis to recovery. With Seymour and his wife Shirley I cherish not only a partnership but also a much valued friendship.

Above all, I was mindful of the immense contribution of my colleagues in the rabbinate. Their work is often sadly under-appreciated. Expected to combine the insight of Moses, the wisdom of Solomon, the eloquence of Isaiah and the patience of Job, they are sometimes subjected to the treatment of Balaam's ass. Watching them in action I have often marvelled at how, day after day, they have brought comfort to the afflicted, inspiration to the weary and guidance to those who search. A synagogue without a rabbi is like a body without a soul, and they more than anyone else are the builders of our community. Like them I owe much to the advice and encouragement of my predecessor, Lord Jakobovits, Rosh Beth Din Dayan Chanokh Ehrentreu, and Dayanim Dovid Kaplin, Ivan Binstock and Menachem Gelley of the London Beth Din.

Special thanks are due to Peter Halban for the speed and professionalism with which he has brought this work into print; to Beverley-Jane Stewart for her cover illustration, painted especially for the United Synagogue's anniversary and showing aspects of its work; and to my superb office team, led by my Executive Director Jonathan Kestenbaum, for their unfailing good humour and support. I am particularly grateful to the incorporated trustees of the Jewish community of Hong Kong for their assistance with this publication. Their new community centre is a model of its kind, and what I have written in this essay will, I hope, guide them in their ambitious plans for developing Jewish life.

It is not easy for a Chief Rabbi to find the time to write. The historian Shlomo Dov Goitein writes that it was Maimonides' great fortune, having been appointed as *Rosh ha-Yehudim* (head of the Jewish community) in Egypt, to be deposed after five years, in 1176. This gave him a twenty year interlude in which he was able to write the *Mishneh Torah* and the *Guide for the Perplexed*. His son Rabbi Abraham was appointed *Nagid* (Chief Rabbi) as a young man, and he occupied the position throughout his life. This, says Goitein, was why his literary output was so limited and his place in Jewish history so relatively small.

The present study is therefore a sketch rather than a finished portrait, and any errors of detail will I hope be balanced by the broad strokes of the argument. The reason I have taken the trouble to write it is that like so many organisations that have been in existence for a long time, the United Synagogue runs the risk of being taken for granted. No institution can survive without being constantly renewed, least of all at times of change of which this is one. I have tried to set out, in a way I have not seen done before, the singularity of its achievement and the vital importance of continuing it into the future. I hope it will stimulate thought not only amongst its members but also in those outside who wish to understand why it is what it is, and why Anglo-Jewry did not develop along different lines. At the heart of the United Synagogue is an idea, one which governed and inspired Jewish communities for many centuries but which has proved difficult to sustain in the modern world. I have tried in this book to describe the history and theology of this idea and to show why its importance extends far beyond the boundaries of Anglo-Jewry.

While working on it I made a belated and serendipitous discovery. I had not previously realised that the day I was married, 14 July 1970, exactly coincided with the centenary of the United Synagogue. Its 125th anniversary was therefore our silver wedding, and this made me more than usually conscious of the debt I owe my wife Elaine, who throughout those years has been a never-failing source of encouragement and love. To her, and to our children Joshua, Dina and Gila, go my deepest thanks for helping me discover what it is for the *Shekhinah*, the Divine presence, to live in the midst of human relationships. That is the ultimate blessing of a community of faith.

Jonathan Sacks
London
Rosh Chodesh Ellul 5755

Part One
House of Faith

1 · The Architecture of Community

Walk round the Old City of Jerusalem and you will come to a strange realisation. The Christian quarter is full of fine churches. On the Temple Mount stand two magnificent mosques, El Aqsa and the Dome of the Rock. But the Jewish quarter contains no synagogues of comparable grandeur. Those that were there were destroyed by the Jordanians in 1949. Most have since been rebuilt though some, like the Hurvah, have been preserved as ruins. The largest place of prayer is not a synagogue at all. It is the open space in front of the *Kotel Hamaaravi*, the Western Wall, symbol and vestige of the Temple that twice stood and was twice destroyed. Since then, for the most part, Jews have not tried to rival its splendour. They built synagogues, *battei knesset*, houses of worship. But often they were small, modest and unspectacular.

Go to Prague and you discover the same thing. There, close to the centre of this majestic city of castles and spires, you come across one of the most famous and oldest of Europe's synagogues, the Altneushul, where the great Rabbi Judah Loewe, the Maharal, lived and where, so legend has it, he created the golem, the artificial being who defended Jews against their enemies. Perhaps its protection continued into the twentieth century, because while other Jewish buildings were systematically destroyed by the Nazis, the Altneushul survived. Entering it you are struck by its tiny dimensions. It is a deeply atmospheric place, and has the feel of the Middle Ages about it. The seat where the Maharal sat is still there, and you can imagine yourself back in the sixteenth century when Jewish life was still lit by the flame of a faith not yet blown by the winds of modernity. But there is nothing lavish or spacious about it. By the standards of Prague the Altneushul is the humblest of public places.

The Jewish contribution to civilisation did not lie in architecture. There were exceptions. But at most times, Jews built relatively modest places of worship, and one is led to wonder why. Was it that often they were simply poor and few in number? Or that neither Christians nor Muslims allowed them to build houses of worship that might rival their own? Was it simply that experience had taught them that, during the long night of exile, no place of residence was secure? Had they been expelled too often from too many countries to seek permanence in stone? There is a measure of truth in each of these suggestions, but I cannot help feeling that the larger truth lies elsewhere.

After the destruction of the Second Temple Jews lived by an ancient and fundamental insight, that God does not live in buildings but in the human heart. When He commanded the Israelites to construct the tabernacle, He said, 'They shall make Me a sanctuary that I may dwell in their midst' (Exodus 25:8) – in their midst, not its midst. The *Shekhinah*, God's indwelling presence, was in a people not a place. The traces of His spirit are to be found in human lives. What in other faiths was achieved through architecture – visible symbols of the order and majesty of creation – was achieved in Judaism through the life of the holy community, constructed according to the plans of the Torah. The rabbis carved, polished and engraved its teachings as if they were the stones of a great edifice, and so they were, but it was a living one built out of words and deeds. A Jewish legend says that when the Temple was destroyed splinters from its stones entered the hearts of the Jewish people. When they gathered as *Knesset Yisrael*, the congregation of Israel united across space and time in the collective service of God, they became a kind of human Temple and in their lives the Divine presence found its earthly home. So, when they were not trying to imitate their neighbours, Jews rarely put their energies into buildings. They put them into study and worship and acts of social welfare. They constructed synagogues, but what they built was communities of faith.

This book is about one such community, the group of London congregations known as the United Synagogue. As I write, it is in the midst of its 125th anniversary, and it has much to celebrate. Throughout its existence it has attracted the allegiance of the majority of London's Jews and has had an influence over the rest of Anglo-Jewry and beyond. When it came into being the British Empire was at its height, so that the Anglo-Jewish example set a pattern for other Jewries as distant as Australia, New Zealand, South Africa and Canada. Even today these communities are significantly different from Jewries elsewhere.

But my subject goes beyond a conventional history of one particular organisation. Instead I have attempted an intellectual journey into what it is to form a Jewish community and to become part of one. Along the way, we will encounter many of the dilemmas confronted by Jews in the modern world, and the decisions they made by way of response. We will reflect on the concept of *kehillah*, community as the framework of Jewish belonging, and on the role of the synagogue as a collective expression of Jewish identity. We will be led to think about *emunah* – the Hebrew word usually translated as 'faith' but which more properly means 'fidelity' or 'faithfulness' – and how we translate that faithfulness to God, the Jewish people and the covenant between them into the institutions of our shared life. And we will discover that in modern times Jews found themselves reconsidering the relationship between 'congregation' and 'people' and asking fundamental questions about the nature of the community for whom the synagogue is a spiritual home.

Jews cared about institutions. They rather than the buildings in which they are housed are the true vehicles of the Divine presence, and they have an architecture – a shape, balance and structure – of their own. Institutions are more than meets the eye. They embody values, principles and ways of life. Their day to day functioning can often be depressingly routine. But beneath the surface, they are our most powerful way of turning abstract ideals into tangible and living relationships. Through families, associations and communities, a civilisation passes on its values from one generation to the next in the most vivid and comprehensible way, through patterns of behaviour learned and internalised until they become, in Alexis de Tocqueville's phrase, 'habits of the heart'. If we seek to understand a faith or culture, it is to these institutions that we must turn, listening attentively to their spoken and unspoken language, their distinctive rhythms and nuances. It is here that we will learn what makes a group something more than the individuals who comprise it at any given moment – what makes it a community of memory and character, or in Hebrew a *kehillah*.

It is in its institutions – the Jewish home, the house of study and place of prayer – that Judaism's unique religious genius is best expressed. The Torah is a code of great ideals: freedom, responsibility, justice, compassion, family, community and the fellowship of man. But it is in everyday life that the dry bones of abstract ideas take on flesh and begin to live and breathe. In Judaism *emunah* is not faith contemplated but faith lived, in specific ways and particular relationships. It exists not in books of theology but in the deeds we do and the words we say, in actions, transactions and conversations. It is easy to find God in heaven, harder to make a space for Him on earth, but that is what Jews have been summoned to do, and our institutions are of the essence of that project.

Nowhere can this be seen more clearly than in the case of the synagogue. Robert Trevors Hertford, the English theologian, once wrote that 'In all their long history, the Jewish people have done scarcely anything more wonderful than to create the synagogue. No human institution has a longer continuous history, and none has done more for the uplifting of the human race.' More than any other framework, the synagogue has served Diaspora Jewry through the centuries as the home of its collective existence, the place in which it rehearses and lives out its aspirations as a people dedicated to the ultimate values set forth in the Torah.

The history of the synagogue is therefore one of the best guides to the journey of the Jewish spirit through time, and the United Synagogue is no exception. What makes it worthy of particular attention is the fact that from the very outset it was built on a momentous if never explicitly stated proposition, namely that it is possible, even in the modern world, in a secular and open society, to continue the classic terms of Jewish existence. This was so, despite the fact that in many other places, modernity was experienced as a traumatic assault on Jewish tradition. How so?

For centuries Jews built communities. As soon as they had arrived in a country in sufficient numbers, they built synagogues, established burial societies, constructed *mikvaot*, ritual baths, and made provisions for *shechitah* and circumcision. They employed rabbis, arranged for religious instruction, and built Jewish schools. Later, as they became more organised, they developed welfare and philanthropic enterprises. So they had done from ancient times until the nineteenth century, continuing the faith of their ancestors and giving it practical expression wherever they went.

But in 1870, when the United Synagogue came into being, the Jewish world was being shaken by a series of monumental changes, and more were to come. The corporate state of the Middle Ages in which Jews lived in autonomous communities was giving way to the new nation state in which all groups, at least in theory, had equal rights. Jews fought for emancipation, which meant in practice the right to attend university, join professions, enter the civil service and gain admission to the Houses of Parliament. Throughout Europe and America this carried a price even if it was never formally spelled out. John Murray Cuddihy has called it the 'ordeal of civility'. Jews had to acquire the culture and manners of the wider society, and in many countries and individuals the experience of living in 'two worlds' produced a crisis of identity.

More ominously, in 1879 a new word entered the vocabulary of Europe: anti-Semitism. It was coined by a German journalist, Wilhelm Marr, to describe an old phenomenon that was mutating into a new and virulent disease. Jews had been disliked and persecuted in the past because they practised a different religion. In the new civil order, however, religion was no longer an adequate ground for discrimination.

Jews were still disliked, and if this could not be justified in terms of faith it would find expression in terms of race. Within two years the word had become a frightening reality. Pogroms broke out in more than a hundred Russian towns, killing Jews and convincing many more that they had no place in Eastern Europe. Over the next thirty years some two and a half million of them emigrated to the West, radically changing the character of communities in Britain, America and elsewhere.

The cumulative impact of these developments led to a breakdown in the structures of Jewish life for which, even in our diverse and often troubled history, it is hard to find a parallel. Until the nineteenth century there were Jews and there was Judaism, or more simply, there was Torah. There were different communities and customs. There were Ashkenazim and Sefardim. There were Hasidim and their opponents, the Mitnagdim. But the differences between them were small even if, as Freud reminded us, small differences often generate large passions. By the end of the nineteenth century there were Orthodox, Positive-Historical (later Conservative) and Reform Jews. There were secular, cultural and religious Zionists and there were anti-Zionists of various shades. There were Jews who expressed their identity through Yiddish or Hebrew culture. And there were Jews whose deepest wish was to forget that they were Jews. The differences between them were not small but fundamental. It was as if a hammer blow had struck the rock of Israel, breaking it into a hundred fragments.

In England, however, a significantly different pattern emerged. Elsewhere Jews saw themselves as being faced with an inescapable choice. Either they held firm to heritage of the past, in which case they had to place a distance between themselves and those who were integrated into contemporary culture, or they became part of that culture, in which case they felt bound to reject or reform aspects of Jewish life. The alternatives were the ghetto and the melting pot. Jews were being called on to segregate or assimilate, and there seemed to be no third option.

The Jews of Victorian England, however, held an altogether more robust optimism about the possibilities of modern society. They knew that there were risks. It is said that when Baron Nathaniel Rothschild won his long battle to allow Jews to be admitted to the House of Lords, he made his excuses to those who were congratulating him and made his way to a small synagogue in Whitechapel where he was found praying: 'Would that this freedom shall not mean the diminution of our faith.' Religion has always prospered in adversity, and when we have most to thank God for we tend to think of Him least. But the great figures of Anglo-Jewry – men like Chief Rabbi Nathan Marcus Adler and Sir Moses Montefiore – believed that it was possible to guide Anglo-Jewry in such a way as to preserve the great principles of Jewish life without at the same time closing oneself off from the unfolding possibilities of an open society, and without separating oneself from the majority of the Jewish people. To a remarkable degree, they were proved right.

The values for which they fought – the unity of the Jewish people and its continuity with the principles of the past – found institutional expression in many ways, one of which (though not for Sir Moses Montefiore, who belonged to the Sefardi tradition) was the United Synagogue. Its history has been written. But surprisingly, very little has been written about its philosophy, its driving vision of Jewish life. Perhaps until now it was not necessary to do so. Its aims were self-understood, and respected not only by those who were its members, but by others also. But there comes a time in the life of any institution when it is necessary to take stock, to reflect on why it exists and what values it embodies. Unless this is done, the organisation and the people who belong to it lose a sense of purpose and can fail to adjust to changing times.

Let me therefore say why I think the United Synagogue and its many kindred congregations represent something unusual and of enduring value. Some see its significance in a particular style of Judaism sometimes described as *minhag Anglia*, or as a teacher of mine once called it, 'Anglican Judaism'. I do not. Style is not the essence of Judaism. Fashions change. The United Synagogue came into existence in Victorian England, and mirrored its aesthetics. The great challenge to Jews in those days was social integration, and at times they emphasised their Englishness at the expense of their Jewishness. They built large and imposing synagogues and conducted services of fastidious decorum. They were magnificent, but have since somewhat lost their appeal for a generation more interested in compelling centres of community, places of personal spiritual growth. Synagogue styles have changed, and that is a sign not of decay but of vitality.

Others think of the United Synagogue in terms of a specific philosophy of Judaism, variously termed 'neo-' or 'modern' or 'centrist' Orthodoxy, whose great exponent in the nineteenth century was Rabbi Samson Raphael Hirsch. This is in fact a misconception. Jewry in Germany and the United States did give rise to a self-defined neo-Orthodoxy. Anglo-Jewry did not. The United Synagogue was not the projection of a particular school of thought. Instead it drew its inspiration from all aspects of Jewish tradition. It was neither forced by Jewish dissent, nor prompted by inclination, to create an ideology. It stood quite simply for Judaism and Jews, wherever possible without qualifying adjectives.

The United Synagogue's great achievement lay in neither style nor ideology but in the undertaking it set itself in its Hebrew name, *Knesset Yisrael*, 'the congregation of Israel'. As we will see, this was a bold and by no means inevitable choice. It meant in effect that it set itself as far as possible to sustain the traditional nature of the Jewish community as a collective body dedicated to the service of God and the continuation of the covenant. Before the nineteenth century, no Jewish community would have contemplated doing otherwise. But by 1870, this was already a brave undertaking, calling for responsive leadership of a high order. It meant declining two alternatives: turning Judaism into a sect self-consciously separated from the rest of the Jewish world, or breaking continuity with the past and ultimately seeing Jewry as an ethnic group which wrote the rules of its own civilisation. Anglo-Jews have reason to be grateful that their predecessors for the most part refused these options.

As a result, the synagogues that predominated in Britain and throughout the Commonwealth remained open to the whole of Jewish tradition and not just part of it, and to the whole of the Jewish people and not just part of it. The individuals who made up these communities were not more observant, or more Jewishly learned, in their private lives than Jews elsewhere. But in their public expressions and institutional forms they preserved the great Judaic heritage more widely and successfully than communities in many other countries.

Elsewhere Orthodoxy was reduced to a small and until recently embattled minority in communities in which the majority of the Jewish population were estranged from tradition. In Anglo-Jewry and the Commonwealth Jewries over which it had an influence, this did not happen. Despite all the pressures of more than a century of stress and change, they have held together as communities. A relatively high percentage of their population are members of synagogues, and the majority – in Britain between two-thirds and four-fifths – of Orthodox congregations. This means that in them Orthodoxy has remained more tolerant, open and inclusive than elsewhere. It has developed a stance of responsibility towards the community as a whole, and not merely towards its own members. It has ensured that certain norms and standards – those which link us to the Jewish past and to Jews worldwide – have stood unshaken at the centre of our communal life. This means that, by and large, Jews in Britain can talk to one another in the shared language of our faith, and at a time when Jewish unity and continuity are at risk, this is an achievement as precious as it is rare. Like the Altneushul in Prague, Anglo-Jewry survives intact where so many other communities have fragmented.

Today there are intense pressures for it to go the way of the world's two largest Jewries, those of Israel and the United States. This would mean a minority Orthodoxy, divided within itself, and a large majority for whom the Jewish past is a foreign country and Jewish faith as it has been lived through the generations something alien and strange. Were Anglo-Jewry to follow this road it would be a grave error. Individuals would be alienated. The community would be split. Orthodoxy itself would lose its breadth, its engagement with the wider world and its sense of kinship with other Jews. The public life of Jewry would be secularised, because the only ground on which Jews could meet would be religiously neutral: defence, welfare and Israel shorn of their spiritual dimensions. Jewry here would be embarked on a course it has already taken elsewhere with deeply damaging consequences. It would be on its way to becoming a secular entity rather than a community of faith.

Against this, I believe that it matters that there are Jews who, faithful to the Judaism of the millennia, construct communities in which that faith lives and changes the lives of those who become part of them. It matters that those communities are built around the life of Torah, forming an axis of continuity between ourselves and the generations that preceded us. A Jewish community should build its standards around its aspirations, holding out to its members the challenge of eternal ideals rather than an ever-changing set of accommodations to passing fashion, moral, spiritual or intellectual. It therefore matters that it embodies an institutional expression of humility in the face of God and reverence for the traditions of its ancestors, never losing its sense of infinity in the midst of space or of eternity in the flux of time.

It matters that there is a living example of Orthodoxy that is tolerant, accessible and open to all, with no other precondition than that in its public expressions it respects the faith and way of life that has been passed on by Jews from parents to children throughout the centuries. It matters that there be a Judaism which, without compromising its commitments, is fully open to the time, the culture and the society in which Jews live, and which has the courage to wrestle with contemporary life rather than avoid the confrontation. It matters that Jewish communities feel themselves part of, and accept responsibilities towards, *Knesset Yisrael*, the extended 'congregation of Israel' which encompasses Jews of all times and places, overcoming the perennial temptations of parochialism, sectarianism and narrow loyalties.

These values are not peculiar to any one community of Jews. But wherever they are taken seriously, they will lead to something like the United Synagogue. If it did not exist, it would be necessary to invent it. But it would prove extraordinarily difficult to re-invent it, such are the powerful pressures in today's Jewish world to fragment communities into separate and competing sects, each going its own way. What has made the United Synagogue so important a model of Jewish life is that it has resisted these centrifugal pressures and will continue to do so, because they do justice neither to the Jewish past nor to our collective future.

The United Synagogue has been much criticised in recent years. But the time has come to reflect on its specific virtues, the attributes which make it, despite its many faults, one of the more remarkable religious institutions modern Jewry has created. Its ideals are still compelling. If anything they are more important now than they were a century and a quarter ago. Its synagogues are impressive, but their significance lies in their inner life, not their outer form. They are a brave translation into the contemporary world of the revolutionary ideal which Jews have pursued for most of their recorded history: *Knesset Yisrael*, the Jewish people as a living community of faith. It is this ideal whose history I now want to trace.

2 · A Fragment of Jerusalem

Balaam, the pagan prophet hired to curse Israel, looked down on its assembled tribes and declared, 'How goodly are your tents, O Jacob, your dwelling places, O Israel.' The talmudic sages, reflecting on his oracle, had no doubt what he meant. The tent was the *bet midrash*, the 'house of study'. The dwelling place was the *bet knesset*, the 'house of the congregation', the synagogue. These were the two institutions which between them would guarantee the survival of the Jewish people through centuries of exile and dispersion. In them the Jewish spirit would be expressed, rehearsed, renewed and sustained. So long as there were houses of study and synagogues, there would always be a Jacob and an Israel.

Heinrich Heine once described the Torah as the 'portable homeland of the Jew'. It is a phrase which could equally well be applied to the synagogue. Here, more than anywhere else, the scattered descendants of a once compact nation gathered and reconstituted themselves as a single people, united across geographical and cultural boundaries by a shared history and hope, expressed above all in the language of their prayers. The synagogue was one of Jewry's most remarkable institutions. Through it they overcame the pressures of history, resisting the otherwise overwhelming forces of forgetfulness and assimilation. Driven from the land of their origins, the synagogue became their sacred space, their fragment of Jerusalem, their home.

We still do not know when and how the synagogue was born. Some scholars trace it as far back as the First Temple period. Others, noting the Greek origin of the word, attribute it to the Hellenistic diaspora during the era of the Second

Temple. But the most probable hypothesis is that it began sometime between the two, and somewhere other than in Israel: in Babylon, during the exile imposed by Nebuchadnezzar's defeat of the southern kingdom. Out of the crisis following the destruction of the First Temple, the synagogue emerged.

It has been a characteristic of the Jewish people that its most creative periods have arisen in response to catastrophe. It sometimes seems as if it takes disaster, real or impending, for the true nature of Jewish spirituality to re-assert itself. With the destruction of the First Temple and the Babylonian exile, Jews found themselves without a land and a central place of worship. It was as much a spiritual as a political crisis. 'By the waters of Babylon we sat and wept as we remembered Zion . . . How can we sing the songs of the Lord in a strange land?' How could they pray when the House of Prayer lay in ruins? But while the question was being asked, an answer was being born. The Temple no longer stood, but its memory remained, and this was strong enough to bring Jews together in collective worship. In exile, in Babylon, Jews began to gather to expound Torah, articulate a collective hope of return, and recall the Temple and its prayers.

The prophet Ezekiel was one of those who shaped a vision of return and restoration, and it is to him that we owe perhaps the first reference to the nascent institution of the synagogue: 'This is what the Sovereign Lord says: Although I sent them far away among the nations and scattered them among the countries, yet I have become to them a small sanctuary [*mikdash me'at*] in the countries where they have gone.' Ezekiel's phrase contained the foundation of hope. The central sanctuary had been destroyed, but a small echo of it remained.

The Jewish assemblies (*kinishtu* in Babylonian, *knesset* in Hebrew) were not substitutes for the ruined Temple in Jerusalem. The importance of this cannot be overstated. It was not that the exiles had decided to make Babylon their permanent home and there build Jerusalem. The prophet Jeremiah wrote them a letter in which he told them to 'Build houses and settle down . . . Also, seek the peace of the city to which I have carried you into exile and pray to the Lord for it, because if it prospers you too will prosper.' None the less he assured them that within seventy years God would bring them back from captivity. It was this delicate balance between adjustment to exile and sustained longing for return that found its most important expression in the synagogue.

In it, Jews recreated something of the lost Temple without forgetting that the real Temple was somewhere else. The reminders were to be found not only in the expositions and prayers uttered in the synagogue, but in its physical orientation. The book of Daniel suggests that Jews in Babylon were accustomed to pray towards Jerusalem, thus preserving the memory of the holy city as the ultimate place of prayer. Synagogues have shared this feature since. But even as they remembered Jerusalem, Jews made the crucial discovery that they could recapture a little of its spirit elsewhere. As the rabbis of a later age were to put it: when Israel is exiled, the Divine presence goes into exile with them. It was a turning point in the history of Judaism. Though Israel never gave up hope of living as a sovereign people in its own land, it discovered that it could sustain its inner life even in a diaspora. The synagogue became the centre of its collective existence. It was the home of the Jewish heart.

A Jewish historian, Professor M. Stern, has written that 'in establishing the synagogue, Judaism created one of the greatest revolutions in the history of religion and society, for the synagogue was an entirely new environment for divine service, of a type unknown anywhere before'. It is a verdict shared by Ernest Renan, the nineteenth century French historian, who called the synagogue 'the most original and fruitful creation of the Jewish people'. Neither temple nor shrine, it was a place sanctified by the purposes of those who met there. It was, simply, a house of prayer. As Salo Baron, the Jewish historian, puts it, it represented a 'truly epochal revolution' through which 'the exilic community . . . completely shifted the emphasis from the place of worship, the sanctuary, to the gathering of worshippers, the congregation, assembled at any time and any place in God's wide world'. Its influence was eventually to travel far beyond Judaism, for it became in time the prototype of the Christian church and the Islamic mosque.

More than any other faith, Judaism embodies the tension between the particular and the universal. It is the faith of a particular people but it worships the universal God, creator of heaven and earth. Its values are those of humanity as such, and no book has been more influential than the Hebrew Bible in shaping the moral aspirations of mankind. But the ways in which it lives out those values are highly specific and particular: the elaborate code of commandments through which holiness is brought down from heaven to earth. One of the most vivid ways in which Jews have lived out this tension is in its understanding of the idea of sacred space.

The Jewish journey, begun by Abraham, continued by Moses, and revived by modern Zionism, reaches its destination in the land of Israel. But Jews have spent most of their history outside Israel, exiled and dispersed. A question therefore arises about sacred space. Is it particular or universal? Does it belong somewhere or everywhere? Is the centre of spirituality to be found in Jerusalem or wherever Jews meet and dedicate themselves to prayer? The synagogue brilliantly resolved the tension. Wherever Jews remembered Jerusalem and turned their faces toward it, there they heard an echo of Jerusalem. The synagogue evoked past glory and future restoration. It could be built anywhere at any time, but it always pointed towards another place, another time. It was the particular universalised, sacred space diffused and transmitted across the globe without losing its point of origin and eventual destination. When the rabbis said that in the time to come all the synagogues of the diaspora will be transported to Jerusalem, they were articulating a deep truth. The synagogue was Jerusalem temporarily in exile.

It was a house of prayer, though unlike the Temple it was prayer without sacrifice. Throughout the First Temple period the prophets had an uneasy relationship with the sacrificial order, sensing the constant danger of external ritual without personal transformation. Prayer had always been both the accompaniment of sacrifice and its most important feature. Indeed the great dedicatory prayer of Solomon at the inauguration of the Temple does not mention sacrifice at all. The destruction of the two Temples suspended the argument, for in the synagogue prayer was substituted for sacrifice, in the spirit of Hosea's injunction to 'Offer our lips as the sacrifices of bulls' and 'Take words with you, and return to the Lord.'

No less importantly, the synagogue was a place where Torah was taught and expounded. Study has always been a religious act in Judaism, and it may have been in the gathering of people to hear the words of the prophet – mentioned several times in the book of Ezekiel – that religious assemblies had one of their points of origin. There is a reference in the story of Elisha and the Shunamite woman several centuries earlier to regular visits to the prophet on Sabbaths and New Moons. At a later date, when exiles returned from Babylon, we read in the book of Nehemiah of the great ceremony conducted by Ezra in Jerusalem in which the Torah was read from publicly and the Levites instructed the congregation: 'They read from the book of the Law of God, making it clear and giving the meaning so that the people could understand what was being read.'

The priestly exposition of the Torah and the prophetic interpretation of its texts evolved over time into the rabbinic *derashah* or homily, which continued to hold a central place in religious gatherings. Philo, writing about a typical Jewish assembly in Egypt, explains that 'some priest who is present, or one of the elders, reads the sacred laws to them, and interprets each of them separately until evening, and then they depart, having gained some skill in the sacred laws and having made great advances toward piety'. The synagogue thus became the community's ongoing tutorial in its own teachings and traditions.

Not only was Torah expounded. It was read, or more precisely, proclaimed. The book of Deuteronomy refers to a seven-yearly convocation of the entire people, men, women and children, to hear the Torah publicly recited. This was partly a moment of national education, 'so that they can listen and learn to fear the Lord your God and follow carefully all the words of this law'. But in part, too, it was a political-religious event, renewing the covenant of Israel as a people whose constitution was the Torah. The regular reading of the Torah in the synagogue, with its echoes of this national ceremony, was thus a reminder and ratification of the terms on which Jews came together to form communities. As Daniel Elazar notes, individual congregations reproduced in miniature the classic terms of Jewish nationhood. 'In effect, every local Jewish community, as a congregation, was considered to be a kind of partnership based upon a common contractual obligation within the framework of the overall Jewish constitution, namely the Torah.' By regularly proclaiming the Torah, Jews reaffirmed its sovereignty as the code of their common life.

As the name *bet knesset*, 'house of gathering', implies, the synagogue was also a communal centre in the broadest sense. The vast synagogue in Alexandria, whose lavishness awed contemporary observers, was divided according to trades, each sitting in separate sections, so that newcomers to the city were able to use it as a kind of employment exchange, easily locating their fellow craftsmen. Other ancient synagogues were organised on *Landsmannschaften* principles, providing a home for Jews from similar places of origin. The synagogue became the place where communal announcements were made, law suits were heard, and charitable funds deposited and distributed. The Talmud informs us that in Babylon places of Jewish worship were often supplied with temporary lodgings where visitors could receive hospitality.

The remark of Israel Abrahams, the nineteenth century Anglo-Jewish scholar, about the medieval synagogue, that it 'tended, with ever-increasing rapidity, to absorb and develop the social life of the community', could be applied with equal justice to a much earlier age. It was the focus not only of relations between man and God, but also of relations between man and man. The interweaving of sacred and secular, already a feature of the Hebrew Bible, was here continued. The economic and social life of the community was brought within the ambit of the Divine presence.

The result was that by the time crisis again threatened the Jewish people, with the destruction of the Second Temple in 70 CE and the suppression of the Bar Kochba revolt sixty-five years later, an institution already existed that was to prove capable of one of the most remarkable of all achievements of religious and cultural continuity: the sustaining of Jewish identity through centuries of global dispersion. It was in the synagogue that Jews were able to keep alive the three things on which their existence depended, *Torah* or Jewish study, *avodah* or Jewish worship, and *gemilut hasadim*, acts of social welfare. It was their school, their miniature Temple and their social centre. It became their matrix of belonging, the place in which they reaffirmed the classic terms of Jewish existence and their membership in the great chain of the generations. It defied the normal categories of time and space. Whether in ancient Babylon or Greece, or medieval France or Spain, when Jews entered the synagogue they were transported back to biblical times, forward to a messianic future, and lifted to within sight of Jerusalem. It was their home-in-exile, their land-in-dispersion.

Nor was this an accidental development. In the synagogue Jews harked back to their earliest central place of worship, the *mishkan* or sanctuary constructed in the wilderness which, unlike the Temple, was portable and had no fixed address. It was this modest and movable house of prayer, described at length in the book of Exodus, which proved to be the most enduring metaphor for the Jewish spirit during large stretches of its history. The people of Israel never forgot its nomadic ancestors, its Egyptian exile, and its years of wandering in the desert, and memory gave it the resources with which to cope with extended periods of dispersion.

The synagogue did more than provide a focus for a scattered people. As Rabbi Joseph Soloveitchik noted, it became a symbol of the human condition as such. We are strangers and sojourners on the face of the earth, temporary residents whose threescore years and ten are no more than passing shadows on the surface of eternity. The synagogue is 'man's refuge from the insecurity and vulnerability' of his existence. It 'should be called not the House of God but rather the Home of God or more accurately the home of man. God is not homeless, man is homeless. God feigned homelessness in order to induce man to build a home.'

No less importantly it defined the nature of the covenant, and thus of the Jewish people. It is quite remarkable that the Torah takes no more than thirty-four verses to describe creation, but some four to five hundred verses to describe the building of the sanctuary by the Israelites in the wilderness. Close analysis of the two passages shows that the Torah intends a parallel between them. The sanctuary somehow mirrors creation. As I once expressed it: in creation God made a home for man. In the sanctuary man created a home for God. The enormous length and painstaking detail with which the Torah describes the latter indicates that the Divine presence is not brought fully to earth in sudden moments of inspiration but only through the long, structured and collaborative process through which the people Israel fashions its life in accordance with the Divine command.

Israel is a people at whose centre is the space we make for God. In the desert it was in the tabernacle in the middle of the camp, in Israel it was in the Temple in Jerusalem, elsewhere it was in the synagogue at the core of community. Jews wrestled with the paradox of the encounter between the infinity of God and the finitude of man. When Solomon dedicated the Temple he said, 'But will God really dwell on earth? The heavens, even the highest heaven, cannot contain You. How much less this House that I have built!' Isaiah said in the name of God, 'Heaven is My throne and the earth is My footstool. Where is the house you will build for Me? Where will My resting place be?' The answer the Torah gave to this most profound of spiritual questions is that God exists in the space we make for Him, and the purpose of the sanctuary is to open such a space at the heart of our collective life. It is said that when Titus entered the Holy of Holies he was astonished to find it empty, bare of all icons and sacred objects. If so, he misunderstood the nature of a holy place. It is not one which we fill, but one in which we are filled. Its point is, in a phrase I owe to James Kugel, 'to open up a space, a possibility in our hearts and in our lives that would otherwise remain closed'. By its insistence that communities be built around such spaces, Judaism made a fundamental statement about its own identity. The Jewish people is not and cannot be a secular entity. It is a circle at whose centre is God.

So Balaam's blessing, as understood by the rabbis, was indeed prophetic. 'How goodly are your tents, O Jacob, your dwelling places O Israel.' The dwelling place, *mishkan*, meant the synagogue, home of both the community and the Divine presence. The rabbis added to this interpretation a further note. They said: all of Balaam's blessings eventually turned into curses, except this. Israel lost all its earthly glory, but it never lost its synagogues. Because of this, it survived. No other people maintained its identity through two thousand years of dispersion, but Jews did, because though they had lost their geographic home they preserved their spiritual home, and though they were no longer a sovereign nation they were still a constituted people, the 'congregation of Israel'.

The history of Diaspora Jewry is therefore written in terms of how a series of groups of Jews in particular times and places constituted themselves as a community built around the synagogue. In the case of Anglo-Jewry, this means focusing on one event that, more than most, was to shape the contours of its religious life: the creation, in 1870, of the United Synagogue.

3 · The United Synagogue

Stories need beginnings, and it has been customary to begin the story of the United Synagogue in the *sukkah* of Chief Rabbi Nathan Marcus Adler on 24 September 1866. It was there, over breakfast with the wardens of the Great Synagogue, that Dr Adler urged an alliance of the leading Ashkenazi synagogues of London. Less than four years later, on 14 July 1870, the Jewish United Synagogues Bill received royal assent and the United Synagogue was born.

Like most beginnings, this account simplifies a longer and more prosaic chain of events. Jews, having been expelled from England in 1290, had been readmitted by Oliver Cromwell in the 1650s. There had been Jews in England for some decades prior to this, but they had been *marranos*, refugees from the Spanish expulsion in 1492, who had made their way to England via such exotic way stations as the Canaries, Amsterdam, Brazil and the West Indies. Like many of their contemporaries they were Jews in secret, outwardly professing Christianity. Cromwell's latitudinarianism allowed them for the first time to meet and worship privately as Jews. So began modern Anglo-Jewry.

The first Jews to resettle were Sefardim. But they were soon joined and outnumbered by Ashkenazim from Holland, Germany and Central Europe who saw in England a relatively benign and tolerant prospective home. London was a thriving commercial centre. More importantly, Jews were not singled out for persecution. Cromwell's decision to re-admit Jews had called for no specific legislation. Jews were not recognised as a special case in English law. The disabilities they suffered they shared with others who were not members of the

Established Church: with Catholics, members of the Free Churches, and other dissenting minorities. During the course of the nineteenth century, these disabilities were slowly removed, often to the accompaniment of heated debate but without the organised and politically potent anti-Semitism that marked much of the rest of Europe. By the 1850s there were some thirty thousand Jews in England. Of these, the vast majority were to be found in London.

From quite early on in its history, Anglo-Jewry demonstrated a capacity for communal organisation. In the early eighteenth century the Spanish and Portuguese congregation had formed a committee of *deputados* to deal with political matters affecting the community. In 1760 it delivered a 'loyal address' to the new King George III, and was taken to task by the Ashkenazim for not first conferring with them so that a single tribute could be delivered on behalf of all of England's Jews. Thereafter it was agreed that the two communities (described at the time as 'the Two Nations') would meet and deliberate together. Thus was born the London Committee (subsequently the Board) of Deputies of British Jews. It met intermittently until 1835, when the need for a more formal structure was recognised. A resolution passed on 11 May 1835 expressed the general sentiment that

> it would be of essential advantage to the Interests of the Jews of Britain, that in all matters touching their political welfare they should be represented by one Body, & inasmuch as the general Body of Deputies have long been recognised as their representatives, it is highly desirable for the general good that all British Jews should so acknowledge them, having a sufficient number of Members from each Congregation to ensure the accordance of their proceedings with the general wishes of the Jews.

With government recognition, and under the long Presidency of Sir Moses Montefiore, the Board achieved significant prominence as the representative body of Anglo-Jewry.

No less important was the development of another institution, the Chief Rabbinate. During the first half of the eighteenth century Jewish communities throughout the provinces had turned for guidance to the rabbi of the leading Ashkenazi synagogue of the day, London's Great Synagogue. The long incumbency (*c.*1704–56) of Rabbi Aaron Hart consolidated this influence, which was briefly though unsuccessfully challenged during the office of Rabbi David Tevele Schiff (1765–92). By the 1840s the broad base of the Chief Rabbinate was recognised in the form of an electoral process involving representatives of congregations throughout the country. The man chosen, Dr Nathan Marcus Adler, rapidly set about reorganising the religious life of Jewry throughout Britain, imperiously but effectively, and along with Sir Moses Montefiore did much to give Victorian Jewry its character and coherence.

There remained, though, the fact that individual synagogues were just that: local congregations with highly localised concerns. This gave rise, not infrequently, to the question of who was responsible for matters which cut across congregational loyalties. There was the issue of welfare and the needs of the poor. Synagogues accepted the fact that they were responsible for the charitable needs of their own members. But what of the poor who were not members of any synagogue? Incidents occurred in the 1790s in which Jewish paupers were left unburied for several days while synagogues argued amongst themselves as to which should bear the costs of the funeral.

Then there was the question of the movement of Jews away from their area of first settlement, the City and London's East End. As the established Jews of London reached a degree of affluence and social integration they moved westward to Marylebone, Bayswater and Westminster and sought to establish congregations there. This was resisted by the older synagogues, who saw in this development a loss of membership, revenue and prestige for themselves. But resistance carried a price. It had been just such a refusal, on the part of the Spanish and Portuguese congregation, to establish a West End branch which had led to the creation of the first Reform synagogue in Britain, the West London Synagogue, in 1840.

There were also border disputes between the various synagogues. Could a member of one transfer his allegiance to another? Could he arrange for his son's barmitzvah or daughter's wedding to take place at another? Issues like these had a tendency to create local arguments, requiring much diplomacy to restore neighbourly relations.

From the beginning of the nineteenth century there had been periodic attempts to establish a broader framework of synagogue co-operation. In 1804 the three leading City congregations, the Great, the New and the Hambro, had come together to discuss programmes of joint action. In 1835 they agreed a 'New Treaty' covering such matters as welfare for the 'foreign poor', synagogue membership and an agreement not to poach members from one another, division of the profits from the London Board of Shechitah and sharing the expenses of maintaining the London Beth Din. The Treaty was an important landmark in the evolution of Anglo-Jewry's communal infrastructure, and paved the way for the formation, a quarter of a century later, of the Jewish Board of Guardians, the forerunner of today's Jewish Care.

It was also the first move towards a 'United Synagogue'. The leadership of the three congregations had already realised that something more than local congregationalism was needed if Anglo-Jewry was to establish a coherent plan for its development. In particular, the need to finance and build places of worship in the new areas of Jewish population called for a pooling of resources and an amalgamation of the strengths of the extant communities if they were to become the midwives of an enlarged and geographically more diffuse London Jewry. So, when Chief Rabbi Adler entertained his guests to breakfast in the *sukkah* in 1866, more than sixty years of debate and negotiation had prepared the ground for consideration of an effective joining of forces between the various congregations.

There can be little doubt that, useful though the encouragement of the Chief Rabbi was, much of the momentum and most of the detailed execution fell to the lay leaders of the synagogues involved. Two men in particular, Lionel Louis Cohen and Dr Asher Asher, played a crucial role. Cohen, a leading figure in the Great Synagogue, had been a prime mover in the formation of the Jewish Board of Guardians in

1859. He threw himself into the new challenge of a union of synagogues with immense energy. His obituary in the *Jewish Chronicle* records that 'So indefatigable was he in doing work for the Congregation that it was a matter of frequent occurrence for him to leave a meeting of the Synagogue at eleven o'clock at night, and to forward by the first post the following morning eight or ten folios of closely written manuscript on the subject of the meeting.' It was he who formulated the first draft of Principles for the new organisation in 1868 and who defended it most effectively before the Charity Commissioners.

Dr Asher Asher had been Medical Officer of the Board of Guardians and in 1866 became the Secretary of the Great Synagogue. Needless to say, a scheme to unite synagogues had to run the gauntlet of much suspicion and hostility. The smaller communities were anxious that they were handing over their destinies to the already overbearing presence of the larger and more established congregations. Ageing and declining congregations were concerned that they might be paving the way for their own closure. The negotiations required considerable diplomacy, tact and attention to detail, and this Dr Asher provided. The partnership of Asher and Cohen was formidable and won the day. The *Jewish Chronicle* summed up their respective contributions in the judgement that 'if Lionel Cohen was the spirit that animated the movement, Asher Asher was the right hand that brought the movement into working order'. And so, on 14 July 1870, the United Synagogue came to be. It had been the outcome of a long process of gestation. It owed much to relatively minor causes, above all the desire to find some more constructive way of resolving the frequent arguments between the larger congregations as to who was responsible for what. It owed much, too, to the general temper of Anglo-Jewry in the Victorian age, established, patrician, and dominated by a relatively small group of individuals, the 'Cousinhood', who shared with Victorian society as a whole a sense of *noblesse oblige*. To this extent it was as much an English as a Jewish phenomenon.

But it also carried within it the spirit of Chief Rabbi

Adler, an unusually broad-minded and far-sighted religious leader. A rabbinic scholar of international repute, he was the author of *Netinah le-Ger*, a pathbreaking commentary to *Targum Onkelos*, an Aramaic translation of the Hebrew Bible. Unusually for his time, he had also acquired an extensive secular education at the university cities of Gottingen, Würzburg and Erlangen. Before coming to England he had already served as Chief Rabbi of Oldenburg and then Hanover. But it was as a man of action, a communal planner and strategist, that he left his great mark on Anglo-Jewry.

Almost as soon as he had been inducted into office, he conducted a survey of all the congregations under his aegis, one of the first research exercises of its kind. This quickly revealed a community in a state of religious disarray. Orthodox practice was uneven, often lax. Only half of the congregations possessed a *mikvah*. There were few Jewish schools. Synagogue attendance was generally low. Adler saw the need for strong and centralised direction to raise the standards of Jewish observance throughout the community.

In 1847 he published his *Laws and Regulations* for all the Ashkenazi Synagogues in the British Empire. In 1855 he oversaw the creation of Jews' College as a school and eventual training centre for a home-grown ministry. He was an active proponent of a central welfare agency, the Board of Guardians. Through his pastoral tours he established personal contact with the congregations under his authority, and through his personal prestige he emerged as the undisputed religious representative of the Jewish community.

What Adler achieved, through methods that were sometimes authoritarian, was in effect the creation of a *kehillah*, a communal structure that spanned and transcended the individual congregations, and gave Anglo-Jewry as a whole a sense of direction and collective identity. Within a month of taking office he had already notified Jewish communities throughout the British Empire of what was to be his agenda:

1. Educational establishments, 'from those which are calculated for infants . . . up to such as are to extend their salutary

influence to the future, by training proper and efficient teachers';
2. Houses of worship: 'it is necessary that quiet and decorum, dignity and solemnity should prevail there during divine worship, so that it may awaken the fear of the Lord, foster feelings of devotion, and promote brotherly union';
3. 'Institutions which are of a purely religious character, and those which are established for the furtherance of charity and benevolence, for the cherishing of industrious habits and useful activity among our co-religionists.'

This was nothing less than the translation into a community-wide strategy of the three great pillars on which the sages had said that 'the world stands': on *Torah*, Jewish education, *avodah*, Jewish worship, and *gemilut hasadim*, acts of compassion and welfare. More than anyone else, Adler had laid the foundations that were to shape Anglo-Jewry for a hundred and fifty years, giving it an institutional framework and a set of priorities that defined its collective existence.

Organisationally, the creation of the United Synagogue was the work of an exceptional group of lay leaders. But spiritually it was the natural extension of Chief Rabbi Adler's vision of *kehillah* as something larger than a loose collection of congregations. It meant many congregations working together for the health of the community as a whole. Jewish religious life has often been fractured and debilitated by an excess of parochialism, each group working for its own narrow ends without regard to the welfare of the whole. This can sometimes produce pockets of lively and intense local spirituality. But it leaves the weaker and more isolated congregations without help, and the totality of the community without direction, unable to plan and provide for its future needs. It was this that Adler fought, and fought successfully. The formation of the United Synagogue was one of his notable achievements.

At the last meeting of the delegates before the United Synagogue Bill received its Royal Assent, the gathering expressed their hopes for the new body they were bringing into being:

> In conclusion, the Delegates congratulate the congregations on the accomplishment of the Act of Union, which they regard as a most important event in the Communal life, calculated to increase the harmony and stability of the whole community, and to assist in the fulfilment and development of its sacred duties. They are convinced that union is strength, and that though each congregation can no more shine as a minor constellation, combined, they can and will diffuse light and warmth, in a degree formerly impossible, among the community.

Their sense of moment was well-justified. Experience had taught them that it is easier for congregations to divide and multiply than to unite. For a rare moment in Jewish communal affairs, better sense prevailed. A sense of *kehillah* had overcome local territorial imperatives. Five synagogues – eventually to become sixty-six – had joined hands and pledged themselves to work together. A hundred and twenty-five years later, the achievement is still worthy of celebration.

4 · A Broad Umbrella

What happened next has been told by the historians. The organisation grew beyond the largest dreams of its founders, not least because of the massive expansion in the size of the British Jewish community brought about by the wave of immigration from Central and Eastern Europe between 1880 and 1920. This transformed Anglo-Jewry from a community of some thirty thousand individuals in 1850 to one of quarter of a million by the outbreak of the First World War.

Needless to say, growth on this scale brought with it tensions, and they form much of the social and communal history of this period. Concentrated in London's East End, the new immigrants formed a distinct and lively set of sub-communities with traditions and conceptions of Jewish life quite different from those of the already Anglicised members of the United Synagogue. There were acute problems to be faced. There was the social issue of the integration of a large Yiddish-speaking population into British society. There were intractable welfare issues of poverty and overcrowding. The established Jewish community tended to respond with an awkward paternalism, anxious to maintain its hard-won position of social acceptance within British society. At the same time it remained conscious of its duty to the new arrivals under the principle that 'all Israel are responsible for one another'.

East End Jewry was not always sympathetic to these interventions. Between the two communities lay a profound gap of cultures. To those newly arrived from Poland and Russia, the Jews of the West End had already become so English as to have become almost unrecognisable as Jews.

Anglo-Jewish life, with its 'cathedral synagogues', its relaxed attitude to religious observance, and its quintessentially English Chief Rabbi ('The Very Reverend') Dr Hermann Adler, simply failed to represent the Judaism they knew.

A German observer of the time, Solomon Herz, a disciple of Rabbi Samson Raphael Hirsch who arrived in London in 1881, remarked that in matters of style there was little to distinguish the United Synagogue from the Reform West London congregation. A friend of Herz, Yaakov Zinkin, published a pamphlet in 1893 arguing the need to 'defend true Torah in England' where 'of the whole Torah, all that is left is the temple' and where, instead of rabbis, religious leadership is in the hands of 'Reverends' who 'neither ask nor care' about Jewish law.

During the whole of the period of intensive immigration, there were conflicts between the East End and West End communities, between the recent immigrants and the more established Jews, between the strictly Orthodox and the moderate traditionalists, and between those who argued for congregational separatism and those who maintained the need for community-wide structures. Within Hermann Adler's period of office alone, the supremacy of the United Synagogue was challenged by the creation of the Federation of Synagogues (1887), the *Machzikei Hadath* (1891) and the *Adath Yisrael* (1909), together with the birth of a new movement of reform, the Liberal Synagogue (1910). It was a period of immense turbulence for a leader described by Cecil Roth as 'a typical product of the placid Victorian era in Western Europe'.

The mood of the times is well captured in a report published in the *Jewish Chronicle* on 22 July 1898. A few weeks earlier a conference had been held, in London's Central Synagogue, on the state of Jewish elementary education. Strong criticisms were voiced about the *hadarim* or Hebrew classes in the East End. Their unsanitary conditions and long hours were, from the perspective of the more acculturated Jewish leaders, doing great harm to the children, making them 'pale and washed out and nervously unstable'. The report of the proceedings provoked fierce reaction on the part of East End Jewry. A protest meeting was held at the Jewish Working Men's Club, described by an observer in these terms:

> The hall of the Jewish Working Men's Club has been the scene of many a striking meeting but seldom has such a spectacle been seen as on Sunday last when the spacious hall was not only filled to overflowing but the passages leading to it were also thronged. The speakers were decidedly aggressive and every point made against the 'West Enders' was cheered to the echo, the wildest enthusiasm prevailing when the resolution 'that we East Enders do not recognise the West End Jews as authorities upon Hebrew and Religious Education' was carried. Men and women stood upon their seats, hats, sticks and handkerchiefs were waved and it was some time before the meeting calmed down again. The watchword of the meeting was 'Freedom from the West' and one speaker went so far as to call upon the East to emancipate itself from the yoke of the West.

Unperturbed by such demonstrations, the United Synagogue continued on its course, buffeted but not seriously distracted from its role as an overarching communal body responsible for developing religious institutions for London Jewry as a whole. It took many decades and much diplomatic activity for the old and new communities to draw closer together, but eventually they did, each coming to recognise the strengths of the other. The United Synagogue represented structure and organisation. The East European immigrants brought with them a spiritual vigour and intensity that had been in danger of suffocating under the rectitude of high Victorian Anglo-Judaism. As the Jews of the East End moved outward towards the suburbs, they formed new congregations under the United Synagogue's aegis, and slowly a new synthesis emerged, less patrician, more religiously committed, than Anglo-Jewry had been in the nineteenth century.

It was a measure of the quality of leadership of Anglo-Jewry at the time that so massive a change in the composition of the community could be accommodated without the collapse of its religious structures. Established figures like

Samuel Montagu and Lord Rothschild actively engaged with the Jews of the East End, helping them to develop their own institutions while at the same time encouraging communal unity. Aubrey Newman, in his history of the United Synagogue, rightly notes the contrast between London and New York during this period. 'New York was affected by a similar wave of immigration, and there too a host community found itself faced with similar problems. However there existed no 'umbrella' organisation comparable to the United Synagogue, and the result was that the fragmentation of small congregations continued unhindered.' New York Jewry lacked the overarching framework of a communal structure, and as a result was hard-pressed to confront the problems of integration and anti-Semitism. Anglo-Jewry, smaller and more effectively organised, was better able to survive the strains of adjustment and ultimately to bring the energies of the new immigrants into existing communal bodies.

The strength of the United Synagogue lay in the fact that in coming together, its founding congregations were concerned to do more than provide for their own future. They laid the groundwork for *Kehillah*, an embracing and responsible community. It provided a central financial and administrative resource able to support the growth of new communities in the suburbs. Where Jews moved, the United Synagogue was there to help them. It sustained central institutions which guided them in their development. It organised educational services and youth groups. Eventually it built Jewish day schools and supported Jewish chaplaincy for students throughout the country. Welfare services, which had originated in the synagogue, by the 1870s had been devolved to such bodies as the Jewish Board of Guardians. But the United Synagogue continued to organise activities such as hospital and prison visitation. Above all, through its support of the Chief Rabbinate and the Beth Din, it provided central religious guidance not only for London Jewry but for the provinces and the wider Commonwealth.

What might have happened had the United Synagogue not existed is best seen by contrast with another Jewry, Australia, which for most of its history was closely allied to the British

Jewish community through the British Commonwealth and the influence of the Chief Rabbinate. Australian Jewry is extremely lively, and since the Second World War has built a Jewish day school system stronger than its British counterpart. But it lacked an overall synagogue body. One of the greatest of Australian rabbis, the late Dr Israel Porush, has described the result:

> Each congregation went its own sweet way, without the slightest regard to the needs of the whole or the views of other congregations, and steered clear of most new burdens. So, many things for the enhancement of Judaism were left undone, because no single synagogue was strong enough or willing enough to undertake them. There was, for instance, no co-ordination in the support of the smaller communities, or the care of scattered individuals; no discussion on the lay level of common congregational problems, and no mutual inspiration and exchange of experience; there was no contact among the various synagogal youth groups; neither was there a centralised body that could undertake the mobilisation of our religious forces and the much needed campaign for a return to the synagogue.

Because London had a United Synagogue, these things were done, and not only for the benefit of its own congregations. As Chief Rabbi J. H. Hertz put it in 1931:

> The coming of the United Synagogue . . . put an end to the spirit of senseless, petty rivalry between individual congregations, with the consequent overlapping in some of the communal activities, and underlapping in others, i.e., serious neglect of those vital services in a community which a single congregation could not undertake.

Hertz was blunt in spelling out the perennial danger in Jewish communal life, namely that different groups would spend more time fighting one another than fighting together the forces of religious indifference. The United Synagogue's success lay in containing this factionalism.

To be sure, it had significant failures. Throughout its history, it recognised, but did not effectively act on, the problem of recruiting and training an effective, learned rabbinate. Its support of Jews' College, the seminary established by Chief Rabbi Nathan Marcus Adler in 1855, was lukewarm and inadequate and the College, despite a succession of gifted teachers, was never given the resources to develop its full potential. Anglo-Jewry was ambivalent about rabbinic scholarship. From the very outset Adler found it difficult to enlist communal support for the College. Sixty years later a lay leader, Sir Robert Waley Cohen, could still be found complaining about its emphasis on talmudic studies: 'The community clamours for cultured gentlemen of whose secular and aesthetic accomplishments they are quite ready to pronounce themselves judges, whilst they are complacent in respect both of their Judaism and Hebraic learning.' Solomon Schechter was scathing about the result: 'Occasionally rumour spreads anent some minister, that he neglects his duty to his congregation, through his being secretly addicted to Jewish learning. But such rumours often turn out to be sheer malice.'

The lack of interest in rabbinic studies was part of a wider apathy towards Jewish education as a whole. Even in the eighteenth century Rabbi Hart Lyon of the Great Synagogue (1756–64) was complaining:

> Instead of gathering in the houses of learning people go to operas, plays, concerts and clubs . . . I have no pupils, not even a colleague with whom I could pursue my studies . . . I have established a Yeshivah but have not succeeded with it . . . There are no Talmud Torahs for children, and what will be the future of Judaism if this state of affairs continues?

The United Synagogue came late to the challenge of creating a network of Jewish day schools, advocated by a succession of Chief Rabbis but resisted by the community as a barrier to social integration.

To many early observers it was simply more preoccupied with finance and adminstration than with matters of the spirit. Israel Zangwill bitterly complained that the United Synagogue 'could be run as a joint-stock company for the sake of a dividend' without affecting the tenor of its deliberations. 'Long after Judaism has ceased to exist,' he added, 'excellent gentlemen will be found regulating its finances.' Anglo-Jewry failed to develop the intensity of Jewish scholarship to be found in the traditional heartlands of Eastern Europe. Neither traditional Jewish learning nor wider intellectual pursuits were given the prominence in Britain that they have held in almost every other Jewish community throughout history.

None the less, the United Synagogue succeeded where Orthodoxy in many other countries failed. It held the loyalty of the majority of London's Jews in rapidly changing times. It kept certain standards alive and at the centre of communal life. Elsewhere – in Germany, Hungary, the United States and eventually the State of Israel – traditional Judaism became the faith of a minority. Throughout the British Commonwealth, it remained the mainstream. Through the influence of the Chief Rabbinate and the Board of Deputies, a certain type of Jewish community prevailed in Jewries as distant as Canada, Australia, South Africa and New Zealand. It was less marked by strident ideological conflict than elsewhere. It was less threatened by schism. It was characterised by a broad traditionalism, flexible in form if uncompromising in principle, and it spoke to a large majority of Jews. Chief Rabbi Hertz was essentially correct when he said, in 1931, that 'the United Synagogue has given its distinctive character to English Judaism'.

What was this character? Certainly there was a distinctive Anglo-Jewish style, decorous and high Victorian, which can be dated from the early ordinances of Nathan Marcus Adler and is still reflected in the architecture of London's older synagogues and the form of its more elaborate choral services. But as we noted in the first chapter, this had more to do with the specific challenge of nineteenth-century Anglo-Jewry and its desire for social acceptance than with the essential nature of the United Synagogue. In recent years it has been replaced by a search for intensity and informality on the part of a generation confident of its Englishness but seeking a more compelling form of Jewishness.

More significant than its style is the underlying vision of

the United Synagogue, about which relatively little has been written. Its aim may have been self-evident to its founders and members, but it needs restating today. For at this distance of time, in a Jewish world which has changed immeasurably since the days of its foundation, we can see most clearly that it did have a distinctive vision and one that needs re-articulation. What was it?

Paying tribute to one of its great Secretaries, Philip Goldberg, Sir Robert Waley Cohen said this:

> He fervently believed in three great truths concerning the United Synagogue: that on the United Synagogue depended the stability and well-being of the Anglo-Jewish community; that the United Synagogue was and must always be that great central 'umbrella' under which *all* who believe in our traditional orthodoxy can find spiritual comfort; that only the United Synagogue can, and consequently must, try to hold or bring back to the fold those who are drifting, or have drifted away.

Its mandate was to serve as the broadest possible 'sacred canopy' under which Jews could shelter while remaining true to the classic principles of Jewish communal life. This had quite specific implications. Geoffrey Alderman puts them well in his description of the organisation's origins:

> Communities which joined the United Synagogue lost their independence, but they gained much in terms of access to the terminals of communal power; and, like the overwhelming majority of provincial congregations that put themselves under the jurisdiction of the United Synagogue's Chief Rabbi, their orthodox credentials were beyond dispute – even if their memberships were not particularly orthodox in practice. In this respect the United Synagogue set a standard; as an institution it was orthodox, but it admitted to membership all who were Jewish according to orthodox criteria, irrespective of their own personal degree of religious commitment. This was the essence of 'mainstream' British Judaism, and its flavour was to be found in the majority of provincial communities that flourished in the mid-nineteenth century.

The United Synagogue was to provide, within the parameters of Jewish law and practice, a spiritual home for all Jews who chose to enter its gates, regardless of their personal commitments or levels of religious observance. It offered, and still offers, a context of Jewish belonging to the least and most observant alike. That, in the eyes of its admirers, is its primary virtue. But that, in the view of its critics, is its besetting sin. It is too broad, they argue, to have any particular identity, any ideology, any incandescent sense of purpose. Precisely because it welcomes the non-observant, its temperature is cool, its philosophy amorphous, and its spiritual dynamic too undemanding to inspire. That was the criticism levelled against it in the 1880s by the immigrants from Eastern Europe, and it remains the argument of its detractors today.

This criticism is seriously misplaced. It fails to understand the vision, indeed the drama, that lies behind an organisation which, in a deeply fissured Jewish world, established itself as a *United* Synagogue, and which took as its Hebrew name *Knesset Yisrael*, the rabbinic term for the totality of the Jewish people as a single entity standing before God. To gain a sense of the importance of this achievement and its singularity, we must step back and survey the foundations of Jewish peoplehood against the broadest perspectives of history and modernity. Only when we understand what routes the United Synagogue might have taken can we appreciate the path it did in fact take, and why.

Part Two
People of Faith

5 · Two Dimensions of Jewish Peoplehood

Jews are a fractious people.

Rashi, the great eleventh century rabbinic commentator, notes that when the Israelites arrived in the wilderness of Sinai prior to receiving the Ten Commandments, the Torah's description shifts from the plural to the singular: *vayihan sham Yisrael*, 'Israel [singular] encamped there.' Rashi, always sensitive to the nuances of the biblical text, spells out the implication. At that moment, he writes, the people of Israel were 'like one person with one heart'. They had been transformed from the plural to the singular. They were united.

However, he detects another nuance. It lies in the word 'there'. There, within sight of Mount Sinai, within reach of revelation, about to receive their call and consummation as a people, they were united. 'But all their other encampments were marked by dissension and division.' Rashi's comment might almost be taken as the leitmotiv of Jewish history. To an unusual degree, it is a story of dissension and division.

The book of Genesis is a set of variations on the theme of arguments within the family. The stage is set by Cain and Abel, the archetypes of emergent humanity. Their story begins in brotherhood and ends in fratricide. The theme continues with the appearance of the children of Abraham, the family of the covenant. There is estrangement between Isaac and Ishmael, conflict between Esau and Jacob and rivalry between Joseph and Jacob's other sons.

The book of Exodus confirms the proposition. It is only the

presence of an external enemy, in the form of the persecuting Egyptians, that unites the Israelites and turns them for the first time into a nation. No sooner has the threat disappeared and the journey across the wilderness begun, than the Israelites revert to type as a quarrelsome, rebellious, 'stiff-necked' people.

It is a scene that was to recur again and again in Jewish history. As a sovereign people in their own land, the Israelites rapidly lost the coherence they had under Moses and Joshua. The book of Judges describes a people that has dissolved into a loose confederation of disparate tribes, without strong leadership and with only the most sporadic sense of collective identity, usually at times of war. The book ends in anarchy: 'In those days Israel had no king; everyone did what was right in his own eyes.'

Even after establishing the formal framework of nationhood – the election of a king, the location of Jerusalem as Israel's capital city, and the building of the Temple – almost immediately, with the death of Solomon, the people split into two, a northern kingdom and a southern kingdom, paving the way for the defeat of both, the loss of ten of the twelve tribes, and the destruction of the First Temple.

The lesson was not learned. Though it took many centuries for Israel to recover from the catastrophe of the first Commonwealth, it proceeded to repeat its errors in the second. The historian Josephus, an eyewitness of many of the events he describes, tells us how the Jewish people had become divided into Pharisees, Sadducees and Essenes, and how, even within these groups, there was constant dissolution into factions. Even as Jerusalem was besieged by the Roman army, Jews within the city were fighting one another rather than the enemy at their gates. There is sad self-knowledge in the rabbinic verdict that in the last days of the Second Temple 'Jerusalem was destroyed because of causeless internal animosity [*sinat chinam*].'

Even in the present century there were moments of division that almost defy belief. Within the Warsaw ghetto, until the very day that fighting began, the Jews planning the uprising were split among themselves into rival groups who shared neither weapons nor strategic plans with one another. In Israel's War of Independence only a last-minute gesture of reconciliation on the part of Menachem Begin prevented armed conflict between the Irgun and David Ben-Gurion's Haganah.

This history calls for reflection. Why is it that, at critical periods, Jews have come so close to schism and fragmentation? And why is it that, none the less, for the most part we have continued to be – in some real and not imagined sense – a single people? With these questions we venture into deep waters, for we are essentially asking about the underlying structure of Jewish identity. What makes us what we are as Jews, giving rise to this repeated rhythm of kinship and conflict, peoplehood and division, coherence and atomisation?

Through most of human history there have been two axes along which individuals have formed themselves into groups. The first is that of history. Individuals are bound to one another because they share the same ancestry, the same ethnic origins, and the sense of a shared past. They are, in effect, an extended family. When they look back they find ties of common origins and collective memory. They are what they are because of where they came from and what has happened to them. This is the unifying bond of peoples and ethnic groups. They are communities of fate.

But since the birth of monotheism there has been another axis. Individuals can be bound together as a group not because of where they came from but because of where they are going to. They share a set of religious convictions. They participate in a common life with shared rules, disciplines and codes of virtue. They constitute an assembly of fellow believers. They are linked not by history but by destiny, by the call to create a collaborative future. They are not communities of fate. Rather, they are communities of faith.

These affiliations are different, sometimes divergent. There can be a single people – the British, for example – containing many different faiths. There can be a single faith – Christianity or Islam for example – which comprises many different peoples whose origins, memories and national loyalties have nothing in common with one another. In Judaism, however, these two axes converge. Jews constitute a community of fate and also a community of faith. Indeed, in a famous dictum Saadia Gaon stated that 'our people is only a people in virtue of our religious laws'. Faith defines Jewish peoplehood, and peoplehood defines Jewish faith. It is the shifting of these two great tectonic plates within Jewish identity that causes periodic earthquakes. For we are a group built not on a single rock formation but on two.

Consider two key passages in which the Torah speaks about the origins of the people of Israel. Both use the word *goi*, which means a nation. As the Vilna Gaon points out, *goi* is related to the word *geviyah*, meaning a body. When a group of individuals is described as a *goi* it means that it has coalesced into a single entity as limbs constitute a single body. When, where and under what circumstances did the Israelites become a nation, ceasing to be a mere group of individuals? To this, the Torah offers two apparently conflicting answers.

One occurs in the great declaration to be made by the Israelites on bringing their first-fruits to the Sanctuary. The passage has remained at the heart of Jewish experience, for it is a central text of the *seder* service on Passover:

> A wandering Aramean was my father,
> and he went down into Egypt,
> and sojourned there, few in number;
> and there he became a nation [*vayehi sham le-goi*] . . .

The other occurs in the wilderness of Sinai, immediately prior to the great revelation of the Ten Commandments and Israel's acceptance of the covenant with God:

> You have seen what I did to Egypt,
> and how I carried you on eagles' wings
> and brought you to Myself.
> Now if you obey Me fully
> and keep My covenant,
> then out of all the nations
> you will be My treasured possession,
> for all the earth is Mine.

> You will be for Me a kingdom of priests
> and a holy nation [*goi kadosh*] . . .

The force of these two passages is quite different. One suggests that Israel became a nation in Egypt. The other implies that Israel became a nation only after it had left Egypt, travelled into the desert, and been offered and accepted the Torah as the terms of its relationship with God and its constitution as a people. How are we to reconcile them?

In Egypt, the Israelites became a community of fate. They faced a common enemy in the form of an enslaving and tyrannical power. Their shared suffering forged them into a distinctive group. The Haggadah, commenting on the phrase 'and there he became a nation', explains that 'this teaches that there the Israelites were distinctive'. The Torah provides intimations of how this was so. The Israelites were Hebrews, a word that has the connotations of 'nomad', 'alien', 'outsider'. They were shepherds, an occupation which, as Joseph tells his brothers, was 'detestable' to the Egyptians. They belonged to a caste regarded by the Egyptians as unclean. The Torah notes that when Joseph provided a meal for his brothers, they had to sit by themselves 'because Egyptians could not eat with Hebrews, for that is detestable to Egyptians'. They were, in short, framed by their experiences of being like one another and different from those around them. They had the same ancestry and origins and now, transported into an alien environment, they shared the same fate. That, in one sense, is how they became a nation.

At Sinai they became a nation in a quite different sense. They became a body politic, with its own sovereign and constitution. Unlike other nations, however, their sovereign was God, creator of heaven and earth, and their constitution was to be His Torah. This revolutionary idea lies behind many of the most important Jewish contributions to world civilisation. It meant that in Israel, and for all those influenced by the faith of Israel, no earthly power could be absolute. Right could no longer be identified with might. Beyond Pharaohs, rulers, dictators and tyrants lay the supreme authority of God and His law. A prophet could justly criticise a king. All rulership was to be tempered and constrained by the demands of morality, the integrity of the individual, the sanctity of life, and the principles of justice and equality before the law, compassion and welfare in social relations. Israel, not as individuals but as a nation in its collective life, its social structures, its political institutions and its codes of conduct, was to become a living example of a society under the sovereignty of God governed by a Divine 'constitution of liberty' called Torah. It was not merely a nation but *goi kadosh*, a holy nation. It was a community of faith.

Had it been a community of fate only, it would undoubtedly have disintegrated at some stage in the first centuries of the Common Era. Israel, as an autonomous political entity, had been defeated by the Romans. An unprecedented period of dispersion followed. For eighteen centuries Jews were scattered across the globe, without a political or geographical home. To the extent that they participated in the cultures around them, they were different from Jews elsewhere. Spanish Jews spoke Ladino. German Jews spoke Yiddish. When Rashi sought to explain a Hebrew or Aramaic word to his contemporaries, he translated it into medieval French. Maimonides wrote his responsa and philosophical works in Arabic.

To all intents and purposes Jews were no longer a community of fate. At the same time that Jews were being murdered in France and Germany in the Crusades, they were prospering in interludes of enlightenment in Spain. While they were being forcibly baptised in Portugal they were being tolerated in Poland. The situation of Jews in one part of the world bore no discernible relationship to their fate in some other country. To be sure, they still saw themselves as part of a single people and felt their destinies to be interlinked. Those who found themselves temporarily at ease still prayed each week for 'our brethren, the whole house of Israel, who are in distress or captivity'. They preserved their sense of kinship with Jews elsewhere. But it is precisely this fact that cries out for explanation.

The answer is that they were also, and defined themselves as, a community of faith. They obeyed the same laws, celebrated the same festivals, worshipped the same God in the same language, and took the same book – the Torah – as holy. They saw fate in terms of faith. Refusing to define themselves in terms of the here-and-now, they saw their identity in terms of a distant past and an equally remote future. Nowhere is this more starkly evident than in the opening words of the *seder* service: 'This is the bread of affliction which our ancestors ate in the land of Egypt . . . This year we are here, next year in the land of Israel; this year we are slaves, next year we will be free.' In a single declaration Jews identified themselves with the biblical past and the messianic future. Whether in third-century Babylon, eleventh-century France or nineteenth-century Lithuania, Jews were part of a story – the same story – which began in slavery and ended in redemption and brought all Jews together in a single collective narrative. Without that story, told as a religious obligation and celebrated as a religious act, Jews could not have withstood the normal laws of ethnic assimilation and loss of ancestral memory. At some stage or other they would, quite simply, have disappeared into their host cultures.

The key words in this context are *am* and *edah*. *Am*, literally 'people', refers to Jewry as an ethnic and historical entity and it has no religious connotations. *Edah*, literally 'congregation' or 'community', refers to Jewry as a religious group. It means an assembly of all the people constituted as a body politic, and the event to which it refers is the gathering of the Israelites at Sinai and their acceptance of the sovereignty of God and the covenant of the Torah. When Ruth says to Naomi, 'Your people will be my people and your God will be my God', she is referring to the dual nature of the identity she is about to adopt. In joining the house of Israel she is about to enter both an *am* and an *edah*, a fate and a faith. For long periods these two dimensions of identity reinforced one another. It is when they begin to move in different directions that fault-lines start to appear across the surface of Jewish life. That is what happened throughout Ashkenazi Jewry in the nineteenth century.

Beginning with the Hamburg 'Temple' in 1818, there were a series of radical departures from Jewish tradition which coalesced into a range of movements – Reform, Conservative and Liberal – whose common factor was a rejection of the binding force of rabbinic law. Most of these developments had their origins in Germany where the battle for emancipation was particularly fraught and where anti-Jewish sentiment ran high. An important motive for these changes was the feeling on the part of some Jews that they had to make concessions to emphasise their Germanness even if this meant rejection of significant elements of Jewish practice and belief. In countries where Reform spread, Jewish tradition, now called 'Orthodoxy' by its opponents, was forced into defensive postures. Jews had known schisms before – the Samaritans of the biblical period, the Sadducees of the Second Temple and the Karaites of the middle ages – but not in this sudden profusion. It split the *edah* into a series of *edot*, subcommunities, whose differences were fundamental.

Towards the end of the century a second set of developments took place, in response not to emancipation but to anti-Semitism. The outbreak of pogroms in Russia, the rise of racist doctrines in Germany and the Dreyfus trial in France heightened awareness of Jewish existence as a community of fate, an *am*, and a series of movements now emerged around the theme of secular peoplehood. The most powerful of these was Zionism, but they also included proposals for Jewish autonomy in Eastern Europe, and for secular Judaisms based on Yiddish or Hebrew culture. In a sense they were the antithesis of Reform. They emphasised Jewish distinctiveness not social integration, and the failure of emancipation rather than its success, but they were equally radical departures from tradition. Jewry had thus become divided into those who saw identity in terms of *edah* and those who construed it as an *am*, and each was internally subdivided into different tributaries and streams.

The story of modern Jewry is the fragmentation of a once coherent people into contending sects, and I have told it in two books, sociologically in *Arguments for the Sake of Heaven*, theologically and halakhically in *One People?* More than a century later the divisions still remain. Yet, significantly, most Jews still feel the pull of both fate and faith. We understand, even if we do not agree with, the concept of a secular Jew, which means we are an *am*. But we feel that there is a contradiction in the concept of a Christian or Muslim Jew, which means we are still an *edah*. If we were only an ethnic group, there could be Jews of other faiths. And if we were only a religious group, there could by definition be no secular Jews. The combination of *am* and *edah* is a primal fact of our identity, and it survives despite all the rifts of the past two hundred years.

Against this background it is possible to gain a new understanding of the particular path taken by Anglo-Jewry in the nineteenth century, and one way of doing so is through a kind of historical experiment. History is written in terms of what was, not what might have been. But though we cannot know what might have happened had Anglo-Jewish leaders acted differently, we can trace the fate of other communities which did choose differently. I want now to go back in time to formative moments in the life of two Jewish communities, in Germany and the United States, to understand how they responded to these seismic changes. In one case, the response was Orthodox, in the other it was not. But together they illustrate with particular clarity the routes Anglo-Jewry did not take, and thus help us understand the path it chose.

6 · Paths Not Taken: The Frankfurt Model

On 1 December 1844 an election took place in London to choose a successor to Chief Rabbi Solomon Hirschell, who had died two years earlier. In the final ballot there were four candidates, among whom was a young German rabbi who had already established an impressive reputation as an articulate spokesman for Orthodoxy in the new age. In the event, though, he received only two of the 136 votes cast, 121 going to the victorious candidate, Nathan Marcus Adler. With hindsight he may not have regretted his defeat, for in the course of time he was to emerge as one of the most famous rabbinic figures of the nineteenth century. His name was Samson Raphael Hirsch.

Hirsch was born in Hamburg in 1808. As a child he had grown up in an atmosphere of communal crisis. The Jews of Germany had not yet achieved full civic equality, and they faced determined opposition. The view taken in liberal circles, both Jewish and non-Jewish, was that Jews themselves would have to accelerate the process of social acceptance by removing some of the differences that still stood between themselves and gentile, predominantly Christian, society. This led to some extreme responses. In 1799 a Berlin Jew, David Friedlander, suggested that there should be a mass baptism of Jews. He made one proviso, that they would subscribe not to Christian dogma but to a neutral religion of nature. By then there had been a wave of intermarriage on the part of wealthier and more acculturated Jews, including several of the children of the leading Jewish enlightenment scholar,

Moses Mendelssohn. Significant numbers in Germany and Austro-Hungary converted to Christianity.

The broad mass of Jews rejected such drastic measures, for they meant admitting that they could be tolerated as full citizens only at the cost of their disappearance as Jews. The next generation took a different approach, though it was to prove no less fateful. Gradually the idea gained ground that Judaism itself should be radically reformed by the surgical removal of those elements of its faith and practice that served as a barrier between Jews and gentiles. This meant among other things the drastic curtailment of Jewish law in such areas as Shabbat observance and *kashrut*, the abandonment of circumcision, and the deletion from Jewish faith of the hope of an ultimate return to the land of Israel – an expectation that laid Jews open to the charge that they could not be true citizens of Europe since they did not regard it as their ultimate home.

The first Reform 'Temple' opened in Hamburg in 1818, when the young Hirsch was ten years old. Throughout his life he carried with him vivid memories of meetings in his home at which the Orthodox leaders of the community, his father and grandfather among them, discussed ways of combating the challenge of Reform. One biographer, basing himself on the testimony of Hirsch's descendants, writes that

> As an eleven or twelve year old lad, he witnessed the meetings in his parents' home, in which the traditionalists discussed the events of the day and the steps to be taken in order to oppose the bold, impertinent actions of these innovators. The helpless, despairing pain that these valiant men bespoke with their words and their destitute countenance, had so affected the boy, that he then vowed to dedicate his life to the Jewish heritage which had been given up by its own children.

Subsequent commentators have questioned whether the situation of Orthodoxy was as desperate as Hirsch portrayed it. Unquestionably, though, this is how he saw his own times and the role he felt called on to play. He was convinced that Judaism lacked a capable defender, one who understood the mood of the age and could rescue it from the onslaught of change. Jewish tradition had identified two figures who had taken on this role in biblical times: Pinhas, who stepped into the breach at a time when Moses' own authority was being undermined, and Elijah who confronted the false prophets of Baal at Mount Carmel. Both of these precedents resonated strongly with Hirsch throughout his life and he often described his role in similar terms. This aspect of his character was recognised by his contemporaries. In its first issue, on 18 October 1844, the *Jewish Chronicle* published an article about the forthcoming Chief Rabbinate election, and commented that 'Dr. [*sic*] Hirsch was known as the author of controversial pamphlets that evinced . . . more zeal than charity'. Hirsch would not have objected. He relished controversy and flourished in it. He saw himself as the defender of Jewish faith in faithless times.

In his first published book, *The Nineteen Letters*, Hirsch criticised equally the practitioners of the new Reform and the old Orthodoxy. The former 'look upon Judaism as a lifeless framework, something which should be interred in the grave of a past long since dead and buried'. The latter 'has inherited uncomprehended Judaism as a mechanical habit' which they cherish 'as a sacred relic, as a revered mummy'. What was needed, said Hirsch, was a new approach to Jewish education – 'to know Judaism out of itself' – out of which would come a true renaissance of the Jewish spirit.

With this work, published when Hirsch was only twenty-eight, a new tone entered Orthodoxy: assertive, confident and at home in the modern world. Hirsch was the first traditional rabbi to see creative possibilities in the new social and political environment in which Jews found themselves. Where others saw only danger and dissolution, he took the view that emancipation would free Jews from the medieval ghetto which had not only circumscribed their rights but also narrowed their character and spirit. Jews would now be free to pursue their religious mission as exemplars to humanity of righteousness and love. The breakdown of the old political order meant that religion was no longer associated with hierarchies of power, and would instead have to win adherents through the force of persuasion alone. Hirsch, bold then as he was to remain throughout his life, welcomed the change. 'I rejoice that the scales hang free, held by God alone, and that only intellectual efforts mutually balance each other, but that no temporal power can interpose the sword to check the freedom of the swinging.'

By the time *The Nineteen Letters* appeared Hirsch was already serving as a rabbi in Oldenburg, a post for which he had been recommended by his predecessor, the man who later defeated him in the contest for the English Chief Rabbinate, Nathan Marcus Adler. Hirsch subsequently moved to Emden and then Moravia. But it was in his call to Frankfurt in 1851 that he was to achieve his greatest renown.

By the late 1830s the board of the Frankfurt community had become heavily dominated by supporters of Reform, and in 1844 they appointed a rabbi sympathetic to their cause. Five years later the Orthodox members of the community successfully petitioned the local senate for the right to establish their own congregation and eventually appoint their own rabbi, and it was to Hirsch that they turned. By 1853 the independent congregation, the *Israelitische Religionsgesellschaft*, had opened a new synagogue together with a Jewish day school where Hirsch's educational philosophy of *Torah im derekh eretz*, Torah combined with general culture, could be put into practice. Hirsch was an effective leader, and under his aegis both the synagogue and the school grew in numbers and repute.

Throughout much of Hirsch's lifetime the character of Jewish communities in Germany was the subject of bitter dispute. In Britain the Jewish community was organised along voluntary lines, but in Germany membership of a religious congregation was compulsory and regulated by the state. Jews, if they were not to declare themselves religionless, had to belong to the local Jewish community and pay its dues. The community, which comprised all the Jews in a particular locality, was responsible for the provision of religious and welfare services. With the growth of Reform, communal life became a battle-ground between contending parties in which the civil authorities were often called to intervene. For decades, calls were heard on the part of the minority –

Reform in Orthodox dominated areas, Orthodoxy in places where Reform had gained power – to secede and form independent congregations at their own expense. Reform Jews had done so in Hamburg and Berlin. Orthodox Jews had done so in Frankfurt. The question now was whether these independent groups could receive state recognition in the form of a proviso entitling Jews to secede from the general Jewish community.

In 1873 a Law of Secession was passed allowing Christians to leave the established Catholic Church and form separate congregations. Hirsch, who had led an independent Jewish congregation for more than twenty years, now began a campaign for the right of secession to be extended to Jews. His argument, in the form of a memorandum submitted to the Prussian Parliament, was simple. The principle of freedom of conscience could not be applied to Christians and denied to Jews. The contention that Jewish communities would disintegrate as a result, he quickly dismissed. They had survived for centuries on a purely voluntary basis, and did not now need state coercion to guarantee their health. As for the view that internal differences within the Jewish community were relatively minor, Hirsch was vehement in his denial. 'There is no wider gap between any of the various Christian denominations than there is between Reform Judaism and Orthodox Judaism.' The proposal failed in 1873 but succeeded at a second attempt, and on 28 July 1876 the Law of Secession was duly extended. Jews could now disengage from the official community. Where, as in Frankfurt, it was led by Reform Jews, Hirsch believed that it was imperative to do so.

He had won his battle with the Prussian Parliament. Ironically, the battle within his own congregation was harder. Many Orthodox Jews in Frankfurt were against secession, among them Rabbi Moses Mainz, a distinguished talmudist who had been one of the founding members of Hirsch's congregation. They now sought the advice of one of the greatest rabbinic authorities of the time, Rabbi Selig Baer Bamberger of Würzburg. On 1 February 1877 Bamberger had written a letter in support of Hirsch's stand. He was now urged to come to Frankfurt to see the situation for himself. He did so, and on 20 March he indicated that he now took a different view.

The Reform leadership, alarmed by the prospect of widespread defection from the official community, offered significant concessions. Orthodox Jews would now be given their own synagogue and facilities which they would run autonomously. They would no longer be asked to contribute to specifically Reform institutions. This was enough to satisfy Rabbi Bamberger that an Orthodox Jew could remain within the larger community without offending conscience or Jewish law. Hirsch was incensed, and a tense and inconclusive exchange of letters took place between the two. In the event, only seventy-five members of Hirsch's congregation followed his lead in resigning from the community. Seventy accepted the compromise formula, and some two hundred remained full paying members of both communities. In 1878, to Hirsch's intense displeasure, a new Orthodox congregation was formed within the aegis of the overall community, under the leadership of Rabbi Marcus Horovitz, a disciple of the great Rabbi Esriel Hildesheimer. A significant split had occurred within Orthodoxy, between *Gemeinde* and *Austrittsgemeinde*, 'communal' and 'secessionist' forces, and it was to deepen in the course of time.

The argument was less clear-cut than has often been portrayed. Though it is often seen as a German phenomenon, secession actually began some years earlier in Hungary and remained a more divisive issue there. Nor were the leading protagonists divided on matters of general principle. Rabbi Bamberger was in favour of secession elsewhere. Hirsch for his part wrote in 1876 that had he been in Hamburg he would have accepted the compromise arrived at there, in which the Reform community which had always been a minority was given its own autonomous institutions.

Bamberger was as uncompromisingly opposed to Reform as was Hirsch. Moreover, Hirsch emphasised that his argument was about Judaism, not Jews. The second and third generation Reform Jews of Hirsch's day were, he argued, to be held in the same respect that Maimonides had prescribed for the Karaites of his time. They came within the category of *tinok shenishba*, individuals who were in error but not culpably so since they held their views as a result of their upbringing and not on the basis of conscious rebellion against tradition. Secession, said Hirsch, was 'not intended as a separation of individuals from one another, a severance of personal relationships with brethren who hold religious views different from our own'. A divided community should not stand in the way of personal friendships. Reading the documents of the controversy, it is hard to avoid the conclusion that, had circumstances in Frankfurt been slightly different, each of the two men might have found himself on the other side of the argument.

Ultimately, though, there was a genuine 'argument for the sake of heaven' and it endured. Hirsch took the view that any formal association of Jews in the context of the modern nation-state had religious implications. Jews were now organised simply and solely as a religious group. In all other respects they were citizens of their respective countries. As a result, there could be no religiously neutral Jewish endeavours. This led Hirsch to criticise the participation of Rabbi Esriel Hildesheimer in the *Alliance Israélite Universelle*, a French-led charitable organisation which included among its leaders non-Orthodox Jews. 'I fail to see,' he wrote, 'how a man imbued with proper Jewish thought can attach himself to a group founded for a Jewish task when its founder and head are completely removed from genuine religious Judaism.'

For Hirsch, participation in any Jewish organisation was inevitably an act of recognition. If it was led by non-traditional Jews, then a religious Jew could not in good conscience belong. This view was to have profound consequences, not only for Jewish communal life in Central Europe but also for the history of Zionism. Some of Hirsch's followers were non- or anti-Zionists. Others, like his grandson Isaac Breuer, took a more positive view of the return to Zion. But they shared a refusal to take part in the organised Zionist movement, led as it was by non-religious Jews. Breuer was active in creating the pan-European *Agudat Yisrael*, a movement which brought together the Orthodox leadership of East and West Europe in their opposition to secular Zionism.

The division between *Agudat Yisrael* and Mizrachi, a religious Zionist movement led by Rabbi Isaac Reines, mirrored the split between secessionist and community Orthodoxy. The issue always at stake was whether Orthodox Jews could work with others, Reform or secular, on matters which did not touch directly on religious difference: welfare, or Zionism, or the fight against anti-Semitism. The separatists believed – and this flowed directly from Hirsch's political philosophy – that Jews were a religious entity only, so that there could be no Jewish activity in which questions of religious principle did not arise. In a religiously divided Jewry, Orthodoxy would have to go on its way alone.

Those who took the opposite view spoke of peace, harmony, unity and the importance of working together in a common cause. Fifty years after secession, an Orthodox member of the Frankfurt community still felt strongly enough to write, 'May the notion of two Judaisms, propagated by the Secession communities, never gain ground. Who would have the heart to cast out a brother member because he has not yet reached a stage when he can fulfil all the commandments? The highest degree of piety lies in toleration.' More significantly, though, they believed that there was religiously neutral ground in Jewish life. Implicit in the positions of both Bamberger and Hildesheimer was the idea that not every Jewish association implied recognition of the religious stance of those involved. Provided that there was no blurring of the boundaries when it came to matters of Jewish law and faith, Jews could work together on matters of welfare or defence.

The depth and drama of the argument about secession lay in the fact that it lay along the line of greatest tension in Jewish identity. It exposed the growing rift between *am* and *edah*, the Jewish people as a community of fate or of faith. For those who chose the path of Communal Orthodoxy and Mizrachi, the Jewish people was still an *am*. Even though it was acutely divided on religious principle and practice, it was still held together by bonds of common ancestry, history and interest and on that basis it could still meet and work together. Admittedly, the Orthodox rabbis who took this view were deeply committed to the idea of the Jewish people as an *edah*. They were no less resolute in their defence of Orthodoxy than Hirsch. But they felt that even in the absence of religious agreement, something still remained of the idea of Jewish peoplehood, a kinship born of long historical experience and accentuated in the modern world by the persistence of anti-Semitism and Jewish distinctiveness. They could not sever their links with other Jews, however deeply they were pained by their abandonment of traditional Judaism. They remained bound together in a community of fate, as subsequent events in Europe were tragically to prove.

Hirsch for his part knew that Jews had historically formed, and were called on to be, an *am*. On the phrase 'And I will take you to Me as a people' (Exodus 6:7), Hirsch writes in his commentary, 'As a nation, not merely a religion, is Israel His'. In Judaism, he adds, God did not establish 'a church but a people; a total ethnic life was to be created out of Judaism'. None the less, Hirsch also maintained that only by belonging to God is Israel a people. Neither the possession of a land nor political organisation turn it into a nation, only its collective acknowledgment of the sovereignty of God. If Jews are not an *edah*, they cannot be an *am*.

Mordechai Breuer, a recent historian of German Orthodoxy and himself a member of the Hirsch family, uses a telling phrase in describing the Hirschian approach to community. He calls it the 'flight into denomination'. As he rightly points out, this was not only Hirsch's position. It was generally held in German Jewry at the time and was shared by his liberal Jewish opponents. Anxious to downplay the national or ethnic dimensions of Judaism, they repeatedly spoke of it as an exclusively religious association, or as Hirsch put it, a 'union of people who had the Jewish denomination in common'.

In his independent Orthodox congregation, and by seceding from the wider Jewish community, Hirsch had created an *edah* that was no longer coextensive with an *am*. In sociological terms he had formed a sect. Sectarian religious organisations tend to be exclusive and demanding. They insist on high standards of behaviour from their members. They frown on multiple allegiances. Usually they are formed as protest against the perceived wayward drift of existing institutions, as Hirsch's congregation was against the Reform takeover of the *Gemeinde*. Significantly, the Hebrew name of the *Israelitische Religionsgesellschaft* was *Adath Yisrael*. It was consciously and deliberately an *edah*, a fellowship of believers, rather than *Knesset Yisrael*, an embodiment of the Jewish people in its totality, righteous and unrighteous alike gathered together in the service of God. It was, as Breuer says, 'a chosen élite, small in number but select, and of a particular, unique quality'.

The gain in terms of religious integrity was great. But the price was high. Orthodoxy in Germany, according to Breuer's estimate, stabilised by the end of the nineteenth century at between ten and twenty per cent of the Jewish population. There had been a time in the 1840s at which a complete collapse seemed possible. It is a measure of Hirsch's success that it did not take place. Independent Orthodoxy grew in both strength and numbers. But its influence was confined to its own members, and it won few adherents from outside. The historian Heinrich Graetz was briefly attracted to Hirsch's teachings in the 1830s after the publication of *The Nineteen Letters*, but the two eventually drifted apart. In the early twentieth century, when there was a movement of religious return amongst assimilated Jews – among them such figures as Gershom Scholem, Franz Rosenzweig and Nathan Birnbaum – it was the traditionalism of East European Jewry that inspired them, not Hirschian Orthodoxy.

Hirsch showed that it was possible to construct a vigorous and self-sustaining Orthodox community on the basis of a close interaction between synagogue and school. Jews did not have to segregate themselves from secular culture or active participation in the wider society. To the contrary, *Torah im derekh eretz* was precisely the fusion of the two. But they did, in his view, have formally to distance themselves from other Jews, even at the cost of forfeiting leadership and influence within the Jewish community as a whole. Independent Orthodoxy was minority Orthodoxy, the faith of an élite.

That is what did not happen in Anglo-Jewry, and its significance is immense. The difference between Frankfurt and London in the nineteenth century undoubtedly owes less to the respective characters of Hirsch and Adler than to the circumstances in which they found themselves. The course of Jewish emancipation ran more smoothly in Britain than in Germany. At no time were Jews directly challenged to change their practices and beliefs. British society was in any case less intellectually inclined, less ideologically riven than its German counterpart, and its traditionalism and pragmatism helped maintain the cohesiveness of the Jewish community. Reform made little headway in Britain throughout the nineteenth century, despite the early formation of a Reform congregation in London in 1841. By then the Anglo-Jewish community had already developed institutions such as the Board of Deputies and the Chief Rabbinate which were able to respond to new social and political challenges, pre-empting internal fragmentation.

The result was that whilst in Germany Orthodoxy was reduced to a minority, internally strong but weak in its influence on the community as a whole, in Britain it remained the leading presence and the prevailing norm. As the social historian Robert Liberles notes, unlike the situation in Germany, 'in England and France the Jewish establishment responded to emancipation in time to avoid serious religious schism. This meant that until the arrival of East European immigrants around the turn of the century, the religious institutions of England and France represented neither Neo-Orthodoxy nor old Orthodoxy, but simply Jews and Judaism.' Given the new social realities of the nineteenth century and the inherently fissile nature of Jewish communal life, this was a remarkable outcome. Whether it testifies to the tolerance of British society or to the wisdom of Anglo-Jewish leadership, it remains in retrospect one of the great achievements of modern Jewry.

7 · Paths Not Taken: The American Model

Meanwhile in the United States of America a second response was being formulated. Between the 1850s and the 1880s American Jewry was struck by a wave of radical reform. The change was astonishingly swift. In the 1850s a European Jewish visitor to the United States reported that there were more than two hundred Orthodox congregations and eight Reform ones. Within a short period the situation was reversed. In 1880, a United States census showed that there were some two hundred Reform congregations and only six which were Orthodox.

How and why did it occur? There had been Jews in America since 1654, when twenty-three refugees arrived in New Amsterdam. As in England, where Jewish resettlement began a year later, the first Jews were mainly Sefardim, the descendants of *marranos*. The Jewish population grew slowly. There were some two hundred and fifty Jews by 1700 and three thousand by 1818. Gradually, though, the pace of immigration quickened, and until 1880 most of the newcomers came from Germany.

Many of them came from traditional backgrounds and they established communities along the lines of those they knew in Europe. But unlike their counterparts in Britain, they failed to build a strong communal infrastructure, a *kehillah*. Distances were too great. The Jewish population was too diffuse. The entire mood of the new land was against it. It was a country of non-conformism and individualism, one which valued religious freedom more than religious authority.

As a matter of high constitutional principle, there was separation of Church and State. The mood of America militated against centralised religious structures, and Jews quickly adapted. It was a land of autonomous congregations. Time and again throughout the nineteenth century attempts were made by Jewish lay and religious leaders to create an overarching communal framework. Boards, synods and conventions were proposed and occasionally convened. Each time the effort failed, or lasted only as long as the particular emergency of the hour.

Nor did American Jewry have strong religious leaders. By the 1840s, of the sixty or so individuals serving as rabbis and *hazzanim*, only two were known to have received rabbinic ordination. Many of them, according to contemporary testimony, were unable to read unvocalised Hebrew script. It was a situation of potential religious anarchy. As memories of Europe faded, congregations felt free to adapt to the conditions of America with little reference to Jewish law or tradition. The transformation of American Judaism in the mid-nineteenth century took place according to no ideological programme or philosophy. It happened because there was no one with the power or knowledge to say otherwise. As Arthur Hertzberg puts it, 'These changes were made by laymen on no authority except their own – not rabbis, but rather storekeepers in Memphis and clothing manufacturers in Rochester, New York, and their peers all over Jewish America.'

Nor was the mood of the immigrants, then or later, favourable to a sense of continuity. To them Judaism meant Europe, the old world, poverty and persecution. America was a *tabula rasa*, the slate swept clean, a land of new beginnings. The Jews who came were not motivated by religious considerations. Not until the 1930s, when the destruction of European Jewry was in sight, did a significant group of religious leaders arrive – rabbis, Hasidic Rebbes and yeshivah heads – determined to rebuild the structures of tradition. Until then, the first priority for most Jews was to Americanise as quickly as possible, whatever the cost to the Judaic content of their lives.

So, in America, sociology dictated theology rather than vice versa. When the time came for rabbis and scholars to give retrospective justification for what had occurred, it could not be other than revolutionary. By 1885 the Reform movement was sufficiently organised to do so, and it produced one of the most telling documents in American Jewish history, the 'Pittsburgh Platform'. Among other things it declared:

> We recognize in the Mosaic legislation a system of training the Jewish people for its mission during its national life in Palestine, and today we accept as binding only the moral laws and maintain only such ceremonies as elevate and sanctify our lives, but reject all such as are not adapted to the views and habits of modern civilization . . .
>
> We hold that all such Mosaic and Rabbinical laws as regulate diet, priestly purity and dress originated in ages and under the influence of ideas altogether foreign to our present mental and spiritual state. They fail to impress the modern Jew with a spirit of priestly holiness; their observance in our day is apt rather to obstruct than to further modern spiritual elevation . . .

This was Reform at its most extreme, and it alarmed the more conservative figures within the community, among them the Sefardi rabbis Sabato Morais and H. Pereira Mendes and the scholar Alexander Kohut. In place of Reform, they proposed a modified traditionalism. Its home was to be a new rabbinical school, the Jewish Theological Seminary of America, founded in 1887. It was to be dedicated, as its Articles of Incorporation stated, to 'the preservation in America of the knowledge and practice of historical Judaism as ordained in the law of Moses expounded by the prophets and sages in Israel in Biblical and Talmudic writings'.

While the initiative was taking shape something occurred to change the composition and complexion of American Jewry: the massive influx of immigrants from Eastern Europe following the pogroms of the early 1880s, some two-and-a-half million in a period of forty years. Like Anglo-Jewry, the American Jewish community was faced with the sudden arrival of large numbers of still-traditional Jews for whom the institutions of Jewish life they found on their arrival – in this case, Reform – were remote, cold and alienating. The emerging Jewish movement, neither Reform nor Orthodoxy but something between, seemed ideally poised to fulfil the role of a new American synthesis. Thus was born what eventually took shape as Conservative Judaism.

Its early years were undramatic. It was a loose coalition of forces from the left wing of tradition and the right wing of Reform. As its early leaders died or retired, a search was mounted for a figure to give the movement shape and drive. He was found in the person of Solomon Schechter, a scholar from Romania who had spent twenty years in England, latterly as Reader of Rabbinics at Cambridge University. Arriving in New York in 1902, he reconstructed the Theological Seminary and in 1913 succeeded in bringing together an association of synagogues sympathetic to his views, the United Synagogue of America. Both the name of the new organisation and its general ambiance drew on the English model. Like the London United Synagogue it would 'embrace all elements essentially loyal to traditional Judaism'. Its aim was 'the maintenance of Jewish tradition in its historical continuity'. What, though, did this mean?

Schechter articulated his vision in a highly significant statement. The heart of Judaism, he maintained, is to be found not in texts or creeds but in the 'living body' of the Jewish people itself:

> This living body . . . is not represented by any section of the nation, or any corporate priesthood or rabbihood, but by the collective conscience of Catholic Israel as embodied in the Universal Synagogue. The Synagogue, with its continuous cry after God for more than twenty-three centuries, with its unremitting activity in teaching and developing the word of God, the only true witness to the past, and forming in all ages the sublimest expression of Israel's religious life, must also retain its authority as the sole true guide for the present and the future . . . Another consequence of this conception of tradition is that it is neither Scripture nor primitive Judaism, but general custom, which forms the real rule of practice . . . The norm as well as the sanction of Judaism is the practice

actually in vogue. Its consecration is the consecration of general use – or, in other words, of Catholic Israel.

The authority of Judaism was now to be neither the Talmud nor the *Shulhan Arukh* but 'custom', the 'practice actually in vogue'. Schechter was not a systematic theologian and may not have thought through the implications of his remark, but it was very far from a restatement of classic Jewish belief. Jewish law does indeed recognise the force of custom, *minhag*, and of local ordinances, *takkanot hakehal*, whose authority derives not from biblical law or rabbinic enactment but from long established usage or collective decision. Custom is a source of authority in Judaism, but a limited one compared with *halakhah*, the set of rules which bind all Jews regardless of usage or decision. Schechter's apparently conservative formulation – a loose defence of the *status quo*, leaving room for gradual change – was to prove fateful to the development of American Judaism.

What lay behind it was a specifically nineteenth-century idea, now generally abandoned, namely that history reveals its own laws. Within the history of a people or a social order lay an inexorable pattern of development, a law of progress, which unfolded over the course of time regardless of the intentions of individual agents. This theory, developed by Hegel in relation to the State, Marx in the context of the class struggle, and Darwin in the framework of biology, saw history as both tutor and master of events. Over the course of time one could discern a pattern of evolution from more primitive to more sophisticated forms, and the proper human response is to align oneself with this process of change. Sir Karl Popper's *The Poverty of Historicism* is one of the more famous works dedicated to the refutation of this idea.

Clearly Schechter had a limited intellectual agenda. He was giving expression to a school of thought represented in Europe by the rabbinical seminary in Breslau and its key figure, Zechariah Frankel. Frankel, an early sympathiser of Reform, had been scandalised by the sweeping nature of the changes proposed by the radical German conferences of the

1840s. He preferred evolution to revolution. In place of Reform, he therefore advocated a 'positive historical Judaism' which would allow adjustment of Jewish law so long as it was gradual and imperceptible. Like the English writer Edmund Burke, Frankel believed that tradition carried its own authority by virtue of its age and general acceptance, and that to tamper with it usually brought more harm than good. This may or may not be true, but it is a secular rather than religious argument, far removed from the world of faith. Even the most modernising leaders of German Orthodoxy, Hirsch and Hildesheimer, were quick to see Frankel as someone who had broken with the classic terms of Judaism, and both sharply condemned his work. But to Schechter it seemed to represent an acceptable compromise between radical Reform and old-style Orthodoxy.

It was an unfortunate borrowing. Tradition has force in and of itself only in a traditional environment, which America at the turn of the century was not. Religious traditions are capable of renewal precisely because their authority rests on something beyond mere custom; in the case of Judaism, revelation and its authoritative interpretation. History as such has no moral force. For whenever we are faced with the question of how to respond to a new situation we need to know more than how people acted in the past. We need to know whether they were right or wrong. If, as Hume insisted, there is no leap from *is* to *ought*, still less is there a leap from *was* to *ought*.

Reflecting on this gap at the heart of Conservative theology, a graduate of the Jewish Theological Seminary, the late Arthur A. Cohen, noted:

> Schechter was painfully aware of the one problem which his view could not compel: as he defined Catholic Israel, history could *educate* consciousness and *form* conscience, but it could *command* neither. Catholic Israel has no apodictic force. It is that fitful, unpredictable, indeed on occasion, capricious response of the Jewish people to its collective history and obligation. Jewish catholicity too often degenerates into the vulgar response of mere collectivity – kinship feeling and camaraderie.

The problem was not immediately apparent. In the early decades of the twentieth century, the congregations of the United Synagogue of America were still traditional. They had fresh memories of Jewish life in Eastern Europe. But Schechter's formula contained no guidance as to how the movement might evolve in the future. As time passed, it was caught in a set of equivocations. What was Jewish tradition? Was it what Jews had always done, or what Jews here-and-now felt comfortable doing? Who was Catholic Israel? All Jews, or Jews who belonged to synagogues, or Jews who belonged to Conservative synagogues, or Jews who regularly attended synagogue? Were there any limits on how far tradition could change without discontinuity, and if so where were they to be found? In the event, it followed a similar path of development to Reform, albeit more slowly. Traditional and untraditional at the same time, it was always unable to develop a consistent ideology or a clear criterion for change. Eventually it split into three: a radical or Reconstructionist wing, a traditionalist faction, and a centrist group that remained loyal to the Seminary.

There was, though, one thinker who carried Schechter's statement to its logical conclusion. Unwittingly perhaps, by placing 'Catholic Israel' at the centre of his system, Schechter had shifted authority in Judaism from heaven to earth. The 'sole true guide for the present and the future' was no longer the word of God, sometimes obeyed and sometimes disobeyed by the Jewish people. It was to be the Jewish people itself, the 'Universal Synagogue', the living embodiment and 'sublimest expression' of Israel's religious life. This change, apparently slight, was in fact a Copernican revolution from a universe in which the Jewish people was in orbit around God to one in which God, as it were, circled the Jewish people.

The individual who spelled out the radical implications was a young scholar who graduated from the Seminary in the year Schechter arrived, in 1902. Mordechai Kaplan was born in Lithuania in 1881, and came from a long line of Orthodox rabbis. As a child he arrived in New York where his father had been appointed a *dayan*. Kaplan was a prodigious scholar, and by the age of twenty-one had graduated not only from the Seminary but also from City College of New York and Columbia University, where he studied sociology and anthropology and came into contact with a new way of thinking about religion which was to transform his understanding of Judaism.

Kaplan's first involvements were with Orthodoxy. At that time, neither the Seminary nor its associated congregations had yet coalesced into a distinctive movement, and some still saw it as the matrix of a future American modern Orthodoxy. One of its first administrators was Bernard Drachman, a follower of Samson Raphael Hirsch, and among the members of its first graduating class was the young Joseph H. Hertz, later to become Chief Rabbi of Britain. Kaplan was appointed spiritual leader of the wealthiest East European congregation in New York, *Kehillat Jeshurun*. An argument ensued as to whether his ordination from the Seminary constituted *semikhah*, rabbinic ordination in the traditional sense, and the community duly appointed a more traditional figure, Rabbi Moses Margolis, as its rabbi while Kaplan remained as its 'minister'. Kaplan later obtained *semikhah* from Rabbi Isaac Reines, the Lithuanian scholar and leader of Mizrachi. Active among the new generation of Orthodox youth, Kaplan played a key part in creating Young Israel, the first organisation to represent an indigenous American Orthodoxy.

His own reflections, however, were leading him far from Jewish tradition. For a thoughtful individual, these were extraordinary and tragic times. The immigrant experience in New York was producing story after story of conflict between the generations. The parents spoke Yiddish, the children American. Fathers studied Talmud while the children played baseball. A non-Jewish journalist of the time, Lincoln Steffens, described a typical scene:

> We would pass a synagogue where a score or more of boys were sitting hatless in their old clothes, smoking cigarettes on the steps outside, and their fathers, all dressed in black, were going into their synagogues, tearing their hair and rending their garments. The reporters stopped to laugh; and it was

> comic; the old men, in their thrift, tore the lapels of their coat very carefully, a very little, but they wept tears, real tears.

'It was,' writes Steffens, 'a revolution. Their sons were rebels against the law of Moses; they were lost souls, lost to God, the family, and to Israel of old . . . Two, three, thousand years of continuous devotion, courage, and suffering for a cause lost in a generation.'

Just such a breakdown had led a number of Jews in Europe to vest their hopes for renewal in Zionism. Kaplan shared their enthusiasm. But this was America. The Jews amongst whom he lived had already made their journey from the 'old home' and were not about to contemplate another. *Aliyah* was not a realistic option. None the less, he believed, some of the same principles that had guided Zionist thinkers like Ahad Ha-am could be applied to American Jewry as well. But this would involve taking the traditional understanding of the relationship between Judaism and the Jewish people and turning it upside down.

Through his study of sociology, Kaplan had become familiar with the work of Emile Durkheim. Durkheim saw religion as a natural rather than supernatural phenomenon. It was a product of society, not of revelation. It was an instrument of social cohesion, a way in which communities expressed the moral codes which gave them coherence and a shared sense of purpose. This perspective accorded well with Ahad Ha-am's translation of Judaism from a religion into a culture. Kaplan fully understood the radical nature of the course on which he was now embarked, and it was he who applied the adjective 'Copernican' to the shift in his thought.

The centre of the Jewish universe was, he believed, not God but the Jewish people. It was the people who had produced the narratives, legends, rituals and folk-practices that went by the name of Judaism. Indeed far more was involved in Jewish identity than religion. It included history, language, literature in its broadest sense, aesthetic values and popular customs – everything that made Jews distinctive as a social group. Nor were there any rules or standards which made one practice more authentic or correct than another. Judaism was what Jews did. It was, in his famous phrase, the 'evolving religious civilisation' of the Jewish people. Even the word 'religious' was an afterthought, added at the insistence of some of his disciples. Despite the overlay of religious terminology, Kaplan had effectively secularised the idea of Jewish identity. As Arthur Cohen notes, he was supremely a 'natural' rather than a 'supernatural' Jew.

Before anyone else, and more profoundly than anyone else, Kaplan had reached an important conclusion about Jewish life in America. Jews might not be attached to Judaism, but they remained attached to the Jewish people. Young Jews were unwilling to attend synagogue, keep the commandments, or subscribe to the tenets of Jewish faith. They were hostile to their fathers, and to their fathers' God. But they were not – as some of their German and Austrian counterparts had done – about to convert to Christianity. They stayed Jews, even while remaining part ignorant, part ambivalent, about what that meant. Kaplan was the first to recognise this phenomenon, give it systematic expression, and take it as the basis for a sustainable American-Jewish community. Though he did not use the phrase, he was the supreme exponent of a new Jewish ethnicity.

Kaplan did not flinch from spelling out the extreme consequences of his view. It meant abandoning two of Judaism's most central beliefs, in God and the chosen people. His system left no room for a personal God who reveals and commands. At most, for Kaplan, God was 'the power in nature and in man which makes for man's this-worldly salvation'. Equally, the traditional concept of election had to be abandoned. Jews could not be the chosen people, partly because Kaplan did not believe in a God who could choose, and partly because it conflicted with the American notion of equality. Election is a religious idea, and can only be secularised into a theory of racial superiority which Kaplan rightly found repugnant. Jews were therefore to be seen, not as chosen, but simply as different. Their 'chosenness' amounted to nothing more than a collective commitment to the survival of the group.

In putting matters this way Kaplan was moving toward an important observation about American society, though it was a contemporary of his, Horace Kallen, who gave it its name. Kallen was the first to challenge the 'melting-pot' theory of America, the idea that new immigrants would melt and merge into a distinctive American identity on the lines of the great nation-states elsewhere. Instead he believed that they would and should retain their distinctive characters as sub-communities. America would be a 'commonwealth' on the basis of its common language. But within it would exist a variety of 'nationalities' – today we would call them ethnic groups – each with 'its own peculiar dialect or speech, its own individual and inevitable aesthetic and intellectual forms'. Kallen called his theory 'cultural pluralism', and it has been one of the most influential ideas of the twentieth century. Kaplan, whose thought had been running on similar lines, applied it to the Jewish context. Intuitively he sensed that Jews could survive as an ethnic group in America because there was no single dominant culture into which they were bound to assimilate, and they would survive, because they wanted to.

But ethnicity needed a home. Kaplan was quick to realise that the synagogue, at least as it had been constructed hitherto in America, was inadequate to the new terms of Jewish group-survival. It was a house of prayer. But prayer played only a small part in his vision of Jewishness as a 'civilisation' or ethnic subculture. In its place, Kaplan proposed a new kind of institution, the Jewish community centre, whose 'humanist-cultural function' would be to provide a home for Jewish activities of all kinds, thus creating a new fabric of community based on 'neighbourliness' rather than religion. The typical centre, as he envisaged it, would contain:

> Jewish elementary school facilities; boys' and girls' clubs; recreational facilities such as gymnasia, showers, bowling alleys, pool tables and games rooms; adult study and art groups; communal activities; religious services and festival pageants and plays; informal meetings of friends and associates.

Kaplan had by now moved away from the Orthodox *Kehillat Jeshurun* and returned to the Jewish Theological Seminary, where Schechter had appointed him head of its Teachers' Institute. Ironically, though, it was once again to be in an Orthodox context that he was to put his ideas into practice. In 1917 he founded the Jewish Center on Manhattan's West Side, the first synagogue to incorporate an assembly hall, a gymnasium, meeting rooms, classrooms and a swimming pool as well as a place of worship – the 'shul with a pool' as it became known.

Within a few years his radical views forced his departure and he left to establish, only a few yards away, the Society for the Advancement of Judaism. This, as its name implied, was no longer a synagogue in the conventional sense and for many years Kaplan resisted the title 'rabbi'. He was, he insisted, only its 'leader', a term borrowed from the Ethical Culture movement. From then on, Kaplan developed his ideas and programmes in an increasingly revolutionary fashion, gathering around him at the Seminary a group of like-minded disciples who, between the 1920s and 1940s, found in him the most congenial ideologue of a new American Judaism. The name he chose for it was Reconstructionism.

More significant was the name he gave to his new vision of a community centre. The Talmud (*Shabbat* 32a) mentions with disapproval the fact that during the Mishnaic period some individuals called the synagogue not a *bet knesset* but a *bet am*, a 'house of the people'. It was this name that Kaplan now revived. He was too much of a talmudist to have chosen it without being fully aware of what he was doing. What was revolutionary in his proposal was not that the synagogue would extend its scope to encompass the full range of Jewish social and educational activities. That, after all, had been the classic role of the synagogue for more than two thousand years. But it had remained a *bet knesset*, which is to say, the home of the Jewish community as it stood in the presence of God. By proposing to call his new Jewish centre a *bet am*, Kaplan was consciously secularising the community into an ethnic group whose activities were no longer directed to God, but to itself.

With this last step the full significance of Kaplan's journey is now clear. Like Hirsch in nineteenth-century Germany, Kaplan found himself in the midst of a seismic disturbance at the core of Jewish identity. *Am* and *edah* were splitting apart: on the one hand Jews as a people, a nationality, an ethnicity, on the other Jewry as a religious group, a community of faith. The two, so long inseparable, were now moving at speed in different directions and could no longer be held together. Faced with the choice, Hirsch chose *edah* and Kaplan chose *am*. Hirsch built *Adath Yisrael*. Kaplan devised the *bet am*. These were the institutional embodiments of their profoundly opposed views of the future of Jewish life in an age of discontinuity.

Superficially, Kaplan's achievement is hard to assess. He was never sure as to whether Reconstructionism should become a separate religious movement, or a particular style of Conservatism, or a meta-theory of American Jewry as a whole. Eventually it became all three. But its real significance, as Charles Liebman has observed, is that more than any other account, it accurately described the Jewish 'folk religion' of America. Jews did prove highly committed to group survival, but without any accompanying commitment to religious practice or belief. They did go on to build Jewish community centres on the Kaplan model where they could meet and form networks of belonging, but their Judaic content was tenuous and weak. The most characteristic expressions of American-Jewish commitment – supporting Israel and fighting anti-Semitism – had more to do with a sense of peoplehood than faith.

In 1955, Will Herberg in his insightful book, *Protestant-Catholic-Jew*, suggested that Jews had simply become more American than anyone else. The relentless pragmatism of America had turned almost all religion into a means rather than an end. Joining a synagogue or church was the suburban way of signalling good citizenship. Religion itself had become an instrument of personal fulfillment, cultural enrichment or group cohesiveness. It was no longer the 'wholly Other', an embodiment of objective truth, a voice from Heaven. 'Not God but man – man in his individual and corporate being – is the beginning and end of the spiritual system of much of present-day American religiosity. In this kind of religion there is no sense of transcendence, no sense of the nothingness of man and his works before a holy God . . . In this kind of religion it is not man who serves God, but God who is mobilised and made to serve man and his purposes – whether these purposes be economic prosperity, free enterprise, social reform, democracy, happiness, security or "peace of mind".' It was Kaplan's distinctive, if ambivalent, accomplishment to be the person who more than any other took the *is* for an *ought*. That was how things were, and that for him was how things ought to be. Judaism was nothing other than the sum total of the ways Jews behaved and thought. This was the final conclusion implicit in Schechter's enthronement of 'Catholic Israel'.

Kaplan's influence within the Jewish Theological Seminary waned after the Second World War. But it remained dominant among Jewish sociologists and communal workers of various kinds, and it resurfaced at the heart of a major argument in American Jewry in the 1980s. As evidence began to accumulate of the decline of religious observance and synagogue affiliation, a number of observers put forward the theory – known as 'transformationism' – that Jewish life was not waning in America, merely changing. Jews were no longer expressing their Jewishness in traditional ways, but they were still meeting and mixing, and they were still measurably different from others. The argument owed everything to Kaplan and to the view that Jewishness has no prescriptive content. By the early 1990s, however, with Jewish intermarriage rates approaching six in ten, even the most confirmed transformationists were expressing doubts about the prospect of long-term American-Jewish continuity. Jewish group survival could not succeed without some reason to survive, and it is just this that Kaplan's theory fails to provide.

Charles Liebman, one of American Jewry's most perceptive observers, has consistently questioned the secular basis of Jewish ethnicity. We are wrong, he argues, to think of assimilation only in terms of individual Jews abandoning their identity. There can be structural assimilation, in which the Jewish community as a whole slowly loses its character and content. Liebman does not use the words *am* and *edah*, but in an analysis he wrote in 1973 his intention is clear. A Jewish community, he argues, cannot be other than one based, however imperfectly, on Torah. 'I understand Torah, at its least, to mean that a Jew must submit himself to a set of laws and practices which exist objectively or in a reality which is not of his construction. Torah is outside of us and calls upon us for an affirmation to which we must respond. If my community or I fail to respond, then we are bad Jews. But if the community, in its collective sense, denies the existence of Torah, then we are not Jews.' A Jewish community which has lost its sense of *edah* is on its way to ceasing to be an *am*.

8 · The Anglo-Jewish Achievement

We are now in a position to appreciate the significance of what occurred, or more precisely what did not occur, in Anglo-Jewry. The same crises that shattered the religious unity of German and American Jewry struck Britain too. The Reform movement appeared in London in 1841, at roughly the same time that it was taking shape in America and less than a quarter of a century after its beginnings in Germany. As in the United States and Germany, there was a wave of immigration from the East which overwhelmed and altered the composition of the Jewish community. All three communities were preoccupied throughout the nineteenth century with the social and political challenges of emancipation. Jews sought to integrate in the wider society, and this placed a strain on their religious observance. But the fateful development which took place in German and American Jewry had no substantive echo in Britain. There was no communal divorce between *am* and *edah*. Anglo-Jewry remained, at least in its public and institutional expressions, a religious community loyal to its ancestral faith.

This was, and deserves to be seen as, an astonishing achievement. Until the Second World War, some ninety per cent of the community was affiliated to Orthodox synagogues. Even today, despite a considerable waning of habitual behaviour patterns, that figure is still in the region of seventy per cent. Four in every five synagogue marriages take place under Orthodox auspices. In Germany, as we have already noted, Orthodoxy had declined to between ten and twenty per cent of the Jewish population, a figure that remained more or less stable from the turn of the century until Hitler's rise to power. In the United States, likewise, Orthodoxy was reduced to a small minority by 1880, and again by the 1960s by the time the grandchildren of the Eastern European immigrants had reached maturity. On the latest estimates it represents a mere ten per cent of the Jewish community, slightly higher in New York, lower elsewhere.

In both communities, after an initial period of devastation, Orthodoxy recovered. In Germany this took place in the second half of the nineteenth century under the commanding influence of Hirsch and Hildesheimer. It did not happen in the United States until a century later when a series of outstanding religious leaders, many of them refugees from Nazi Europe, made their way there and for the first time provided American Jewry with a powerful traditional rabbinic presence. Hasidic leaders like the Lubavitcher Rebbe, Rabbi Menahem Mendel Schneersohn, together with yeshivah heads of the calibre of Rabbis Joseph Soloveitchik, Aaron Kotler and Isaac Hutner, gave American Orthodoxy a poise and presence it had hitherto lacked. They built yeshivot and schools, set new standards of spirituality and scholarship, and succeeded in laying the foundations for the renaissance of Torah Judaism in a country which had previously been seen as a *trefa medine*, an 'unclean land'.

The history of German Jewry after the 1850s and American Jewry after the 1950s proved one thing: that traditional Judaism is not an inevitable casualty of the open society. Given time to prepare its defences, it is perfectly capable of holding its own, and indeed of emerging with renewed vigour. The tragedy of both communities is that the traditional leadership was not prepared for the challenge in the early and most critical years. By the time it had reasserted itself, a whole generation had been lost. Orthodoxy was reduced to a minority and had forfeited the leadership of the Jewish community as a whole. The position in both cases was unrecoverable. Orthodoxy was left to strengthen its own most immediate constituency and had no choice other than to construct itself as a series of *edot*, enclosed and separatist congregations.

There was an alternative approach in both countries. In

Germany it took the form of *Gemeinde* Orthodoxy. In America it became known as Modern or Centrist Orthodoxy. Like the members of Mizrachi within the Zionist movement, those who chose this path were willing to work with others in broader communal endeavours. They were driven by a sense of the centrality of peoplehood in Judaism. They feared the damaging effects of schism. They sensed that without their participation, Jewish life would become more, and more rapidly, detraditionalised. They believed that collective Jewish activity should not proceed in the absence of a voice from tradition, and they believed that they could exercise a moderating influence, if not controlling authority, from within. But they had forfeited their most compelling argument. They could no longer claim to be building a community-wide *kehillah* on traditional lines. As a minority, they could only lay claim to small and intangible gains, a concession here, a softening of hostility there. Meanwhile the price they had to pay was large and always visible. They were co-operating with, and apparently lending their sanction to, groups who opposed everything they held most dear. They could not but appear to the separatists as diluters of the faith, appeasers playing a game already lost. At the most critical period, Orthodoxy had sacrificed its position of leadership in German and American Jewry, and in the Zionist movement as well.

What made Anglo-Jewry different is that, by the time crisis occurred, strong communal leadership was already in place. At least the structures were in position. The Board of Deputies had been in existence since 1760. It had functioned for years in only the most intermittent way. But when the time came in the 1830s for a more active representation of the Jewish community, the framework was in place and could be strengthened. The Chief Rabbinate, or at least the *de facto* recognition of the Rabbi of the Great Synagogue as leader of the community, had been a feature of Anglo-Jewish life since the early days of the Ashkenazi settlement. Since the time of Aaron Hart in the early eighteenth century, provincial communities had turned to the Great Synagogue for guidance. Solomon Hirschell, who took up office in 1802, was already known in non-Jewish circles as the 'High Priest' of British

Jews, and his authority extended as far as Australia, New Zealand and South Africa. By the time Nathan Marcus Adler became Chief Rabbi in 1845, the prestige of the office was already well established, and he was able to embark immediately on a far-reaching and comprehensive re-organisation of the community.

Structures matter. They make the difference between community and chaos. Anglo-Jewry was unlike both Germany and the United States. In Germany, the organisational framework of Jewry was partially dictated by the State. This meant that the struggle for emancipation was played out in the form of bitter battles within the Jewish community on which the civil authorities were often called to adjudicate. Internal and external politics were inextricable, to the detriment of communal unity. In Britain, by contrast, the Jewish community was from the outset organised along voluntary lines. There could be individual differences of approach towards emancipation without these necessarily leading to the creation of factions within the community.

The fact that Anglo-Jewry had to finance its services, recruit its members, and maintain cohesiveness, without access to government-sanctioned coercion led it to develop its own ethic of leadership and governance. Ultimately this proved beneficial, at least to its powers of organisation. In the nineteenth century, the great patrician families – the Rothschilds, Goldsmids, Samuels and Montefiores, the so-called 'Cousinhood' – were drawn into the service of the Jewish community. Aristocratic and autocratic though they sometimes were, they had skill and judgment and they lent Jewry as a whole a dignity and self-respect that stood in stark contrast to the more traumatic reactions of Jews in Germany. In the twentieth century, as the more established Jews were outnumbered by the new immigrants, the community slowly evolved towards more democratic and religiously intensive forms. Like the British constitution, Anglo-Jewish governance was at times eccentric, depending as much on unwritten conventions and personal relationships as on formal rules, but by and large it worked.

American Jewry, by contrast, failed to evolve a communal

framework. It was as old as Anglo-Jewry, and it too was organised on a voluntary basis. But the early settlers failed to lay the foundations of a *kehillah*, and by the time it became urgent it was already too late. Religious divisions were too deep. The principle of congregational autonomy was already entrenched. In 1855, an attempt by the Orthodox rabbi Isaac Leeser and the Reform leader Isaac Mayer Wise to heal the breach ended in acrimony. By the time national Jewish organisations were formed, from the 1870s onward, the community was irreparably split into three, Orthodox, Conservative and Reform, and the divisions were to multiply over time.

Even the attempt to organise the Orthodox community along European lines ended in abysmal failure. In 1888 a group of New York synagogues joined to form the Association of the American Hebrew Congregations. They invited a distinguished rabbinic scholar from Vilna, Rabbi Jacob Joseph, to become their Chief Rabbi. One of his first acts was to attempt to bring order to *kashrut* in the city. Pandemonium ensued. Jewish radicals resented the imposition of authority. So too did the slaughterers and butchers. Hungarian and Galician Jews, antagonised by the prospect of Lithuanian dominance, counter-attacked by appointing their own Chief Rabbi, Joshua Segal. Not to be outdone, a group of Hasidic communities gathered under a third leader, Rabbi Hayim Vidrowitz from Moscow, outside whose headquarters hung a sign, 'Chief Rabbi of America'. When asked who had conferred this title on him, he is reported to have replied, 'The sign painter'. Rivalry intensified. The original Association declined. Rabbi Jacob Joseph was reduced to sickness and poverty. It was an American-Jewish tragedy and proved to all concerned that *kehillah*-wide structures were now beyond reach.

The existence of a Chief Rabbinate in Britain was a vital force for restraint in a period when, throughout most of Europe and America, the citadels of tradition had been overrun by radical secularism or reform. No one recognised this more acutely than the American Reform leader, Isaac Mayer Wise. He had already been opposed by the traditionalists in his own congregation in Albany, New York. There had been a fistfight between himself and the synagogue's president on the pulpit on Yom Kippur in 1849. Wise did not want to be checked in his development of a new American Judaism, to which he gave the name *Minhag America*. Arthur Hertzberg reports of him that 'he hated the old-school lay leaders, the *parnassim*, who continued to direct the Jewish communities in Europe' and 'thanked God that "in America, there were no petty tyrants, like the chief rabbis of England and Germany," to rule over less well-placed Jewish clerics.' From his perspective he was right. Had there been in America some communal authority he would have been less free to rewrite the script of Judaism. When Chief Rabbi Nathan Marcus Adler died on 21 January 1890 the *Jewish Chronicle*, not always a sympathetic voice, was moved to acknowledge that 'Had a man of smaller ability and with a less commanding personality occupied the Rabbinical chair, it is probable that the wholesale reforms and the undesirable extravagances that characterise American Judaism would have found their way into our community.'

As this tribute implies, personalities counted as well as structures. Anglo-Jewry was fortunate in being led by a figure of the stature of Adler. Five years older than Hirsch, he brought to his leadership not only the unimpeachable authority of his scholarship but also a robust and far-sighted approach to communal organisation. From his earliest initiatives – the survey of congregations throughout the country and his 1847 *Regulations* for the conduct of synagogues under his aegis – he displayed a firm grasp of the needs of the community. As Bill Williams notes in his study of Manchester Jewry, Adler's concentration of power within his office was the result of careful reflection on the condition of the community. 'A "well-regulated" decentralised rabbinical structure had been possible in Germany, he believed, because it had evolved over centuries, but in England a rabbinical tradition was lacking, except at the centre, and this central control had become necessary to the survival of an Orthodox framework of Jewish life.' The laxity of religious observance and the weakness of Jewish education that he found on his arrival led him to the conclusion that leaving congregations to go their own way would be opening the door to the growth of Reform.

At the same time, he understood that mere reliance on authority would be futile. One of the most vociferous points of contention in early Victorian Jewry was the aesthetics of the synagogue service. Complaints had been heard throughout the first half of the nineteenth century, and concern for more decorous worship had been to the fore among those who broke away to form the first Reform congregation, the West London Synagogue, in 1841. The response of the communal leadership at the time had been to issue what was formally styled a 'caution' but which was virtually a ban of excommunication against its members.

Adler's approach was different. To the greatest extent possible within Jewish law, he encouraged a new approach to decorum within his own congregations. He banned very young children from attending services. He discouraged the sale of *mitzvot* and the announcement of monetary offerings. He forbade congregants to chatter or leave their places during the prayers. He encouraged the introduction of all-male choirs. In response to a request from a West End congregation, he permitted Shabbat and festival morning services to be divided with a break in the middle. The result, as Cecil Roth has said, was that 'without the slightest deviation from Orthodox requirements, a considerable part of what had been the demands of the Reformers was met, in fact if not in form'. It was an important gesture. Not only did it address a widely felt need. It served to convince the community that their spiritual leader understood their concerns and was prepared to act when it was possible for him to do so. This gave all the more force to the occasions on which he had to say no. Even his critics were forced to acknowledge that the concessions he refused to make were unavailable to him within the terms of the *halakhah*.

No less important was the example set by Anglo-Jewry's leading lay representative during this period, Sir Moses Montefiore. Whatever the successes or failures of his long presidency of the Board of Deputies and his many trips abroad on behalf of world Jewry, he presented Anglo-Jewry with a remarkable role-model. Here was a successful businessman, related by marriage to the Rothschilds, held in high regard by non-Jewish society and knighted by Queen Victoria, who was none the less steadfast in his religious observance, a man who would rise at six on a Shabbat morning to walk the long distance from his home in Park Lane to the Bevis Marks synagogue in the City, and who in later life would take his own *shochet* with him on his travels to ensure the *kashrut* of his food.

Mordechai Breuer, reflecting on the success of Samson Raphael Hirsch's programme of Jewish education, argues that it had little to do with the theory of *Torah im derekh eretz* expounded in his writings. It had far more to do with the living examples of synthesis represented by the teachers at his school. Role-models were more powerful than ideology, and this surely is Montefiore's significance. At a time when it was being argued elsewhere that social acceptance and traditional Judaism were incompatible, he stood as a living embodiment of both, a man to whom *The Times* devoted long and glowing editorials on his ninety-ninth and hundredth birthdays, commending him as one who had shown throughout his life 'that fervent Judaism and patriotic citizenship are absolutely consistent with one another'. It was just this kind of life that had been set forth as a possibility in Hirsch's *The Nineteen Letters*. German Jewry had the book. Anglo-Jewry had the person.

Needless to say, the Jewish community in Britain had its conflicts and failures. Recent historians have presented a quite different picture to the conventional image of Anglo-Jewry as placid and untroubled. There were deep resentments at the dominance of the 'Cousinhood' and the seemingly absolute power wielded by Chief Rabbis. There were rifts. New Reform congregations were started in Manchester and Bradford even in Nathan Marcus Adler's day. The United Synagogue failed to respond quickly and sensitively enough to the needs of East European, East London Jewry in the 1880s, and so the rival Federation of Synagogues was born. A fierce argument over *shechitah* in the 1890s led to a damaging conflict between Chief Rabbi Hermann Adler and the leadership of the *Machzikei Hadath* congregation, in which leading rabbinic authorities abroad were involved. In 1910 a group of thirty immigrant rabbis met in Leeds to express their disquiet at the drift in religious standards throughout the community. In 1911, after Hermann Adler's death, the view was publicly expressed that 'the Chief Rabbinate . . . has gone to pieces'. It took the considerable gifts and indefatigable energies of the new Chief Rabbi, Joseph Hertz, to restore the situation.

Anglo-Jewry had many failings. Its levels of religious observance were low. Its reservoirs of scholarship were meagre. It had neither the rabbinic traditions of Germany nor the sheer numbers of American Jewry. It produced no new systems, ideologies or philosophies. Despite the intense prompting of Nathan Marcus Adler, for almost a century it refused to regard Jewish education as a priority other than to Anglicise the children of the immigrants and render them fit for employment. Adler himself complained bitterly about the 'gentlemen who tremble at the idea of an exclusive Jewish school and think it injurious to our present or future social position'. Visitors to Anglo-Jewry were caustic about its complacency, its anti-intellectualism and its indifference to matters of the spirit. Chaim Weizmann, arriving in Manchester in 1904, declared, 'Materialist, commercial England has succeeded in burning out everything exalted in our Jews, so that the creation of a Jewish intelligentsia here has become an impossible task'. Ahad Ha-am described the Anglo-Jewish community 'a cemetery with pretty gravestones'. Those who were used to the internal wars of other communities and the heat they engendered found Anglo-Jewry at best lukewarm.

Behind this, though, lay one reality whose impressiveness grows with the passing of the years. Without being by any standards exceptionally religious, Anglo-Jewry kept faith with the classic religious terms of its heritage. With few exceptions, it did not revolt into secularity. It did not rewrite the rules of Judaism. And it did not redefine itself into a merely ethnic community. The *am* did not cease to be an *edah*. Anglo-Jewry remained a community of faith.

Faced with a choice between the paths of Hirsch on the one

hand, Schechter and Kaplan on the other, there is no doubt which way Anglo-Jewry's religious leaders would have turned. They would have chosen the way of Hirsch. They knew that Judaism was, is and can only be a religious faith, and that faith itself – *emunah* – means fidelity to the covenant accepted at Sinai and transmitted across the generations. Revealingly it was Chief Rabbi Hertz, a graduate of the Jewish Theological Seminary, who most closely resembled Hirsch in his passionate defence of *Torah min ha-shamayim*, 'Torah from heaven', when it came under attack. In *The New Paths* (1926) and his *Pentateuch*, a brilliant summation of classic commentary and modern scholarship, Hertz defended traditional faith from its critics and made it clear that he rejected any compromise or adaptation. His predecessor Hermann Adler did likewise in the controversy at the Hampstead Synagogue in 1892, as did Sir Israel Brodie when the question arose as to whether the United Synagogue could develop along Conservative lines. They were guardians of the heritage of Sinai, and they held firm.

But so too did other Orthodox leaders elsewhere. Anglo-Jewry's singular achievement was that it kept faith at the centre of community as the tabernacle had once stood at the centre of the camp. In any other age this would not have been unusual. It is what Jews had always done or tried to do, whether in ancient Israel or exilic Babylon or any of the countries of their dispersion. But in the nineteenth and twentieth centuries it became so rare as to be remarkable. Elsewhere there were Reform, Liberal and Conservative Jews, secular Jews in a rainbow variety of shadings, socialist, anarchist, culturalist, autonomist and integrationist, and there were cultural, pragmatic and utopian Zionists, each redrafting the constitution of Jewish life and in the process weakening the solidarity between Jews, their past, their traditions, and one another. Some emphasised *am*, Jewish peoplehood. Others emphasised *edah*, Judaism as a faith. But none could deny that the living temple which was the Jewish community lay in ruins. They argued merely over what was to be saved. In Britain, despite the tensions and exceptions, the community as such remained intact.

Too little attention has been paid to this achievement. Historians tend to notice it and then explain it away as the product of external factors. For them it had less to do with Jews, their loyalty and their communal leadership than with British society and its unusual character. This may be part of the explanation, but it cannot be all, for it ignores an important point. Germany and America were utterly different from one another. Yet their respective Jewries developed in strikingly similar ways.

In Germany religion was closely related to the State. In America there was a principled separation of Church and State. In Germany membership of the Jewish community was compulsory. In America it was wholly voluntary. Germany had a strong national culture and a sense of its own history and continuity. America was pluralist from the outset, valuing religious and ethnic diversity and giving it constitutional protection. In Germany Jews had to fight for emancipation. In America they did not. Germany was used to strong central religious institutions. America was a land of freely constructed independent congregations. In Germany Jews had to struggle for the right to secede from the organised Jewish community. In America there was no organised Jewish community from which to secede. In Germany anti-Semitism played a central part in Jewish-gentile relations. In America it did not.

Whichever factor we regard as crucial, if it was present in Germany it was absent in America and vice versa. Yet in relation to the development of Jewish life the two communities have more in common with one another than they have with Anglo-Jewry. In both countries Orthodoxy was reduced to a minority and there was a predominance of Reform. In Anglo-Jewry the opposite was the case. It is hard to avoid the conclusion that external factors alone were not decisive. Whether it was the structure of the community, or the wisdom of its leaders, or the sheer loyalty of the majority of Jews, the synagogue stood firm in Anglo-Jewry on its ancient religious foundations in a way that it did not elsewhere.

Individual Jews in Britain had their differences with the community. They protested, they left, they disaffiliated, and in extreme cases they converted or married out of the faith or both. They did so, as far as we can tell, not less and not more than Jews elsewhere. But they did so as individuals. They did not do so as a community. When they identified with the community, whatever their private doubts and hesitations, they respected its long history and religious integrity. They did not seek to reform or reconstruct it. When they stood within its precincts they knew that the ground on which they stood was holy. The result was that though individuals left, the community remained as guardian and living embodiment of Jewish faith.

The question is, what significance does this have?

9 · Belonging and Believing

Dean Inge once defined religion as 'what an individual does with his own solitude'. This is one view of the nature of spirituality, and it has deep roots in western civilisation. Plotinus spoke of 'the flight of the alone to the Alone'. Epictetus wrote of the experience that comes upon a person when he shuts himself away from human company and there in isolation discovers that he is not alone, 'but God is within'. Faith, for them, was something encountered in the privacy of the soul, in the secret fastnesses of lonely meditation. Walter Savage Landor called solitude 'the audience chamber of God' and Aldous Huxley wrote that 'The more powerful and original a mind, the more it will incline towards the religion of solitude.' There are religious traditions built around such private experiences. But they are not Judaism.

The Torah begins with creation. In a majestic series of phases the universe unfolds to the repeated declaration, 'And God said, Let there be . . . And there was . . . And God saw that it was good.' Only one aspect is described as not good: 'It is not good for man to be alone.' Solitude, for the Torah, is not humanity's highest state, nor is it the condition in which we come most fully into the presence of God. The individual must share his life with others. The Torah is a book about persons-in-relation, about marriages, families, tribes, an emergent nation, a people. It recognises that relationships are rarely smooth. The Torah's narratives are often painful. They tell a story of conflicts, rivalries, jealousies, antagonisms, rifts, murmurings and rebellions. In our collective life we seldom if ever reach the serenity that sometimes comes upon an individual when, alone, he or she contemplates the universe. None the less it is here that we must struggle to make a space for God. Judaism is not a religion of the lonely man or woman of faith. It is a covenant which calls into being a community of faith. What is it that leads some religions to find truth in solitude, and why does Judaism reject that route?

Religion has often been humanity's most profound source of consolation. It is hard to live long in the company of society without deep disillusionment. The Hebrew Bible contains a book which perfectly expresses this mood: the book of *Kohelet*, Ecclesiastes. Its author has explored all avenues of human happiness – wealth, power, the pursuit of knowledge – and seen that they end in grief. Wealth dies with us. Fame is fleeting. Wisdom is briefly acknowledged, then forgotten. Justice withers under the relentless onslaught of power. Beneath the sun, human striving seems futile, empty, destined to failure. Faced with the apparent arbitrariness of the world, the individual driven by a glimpse of perfection can come to find it in an alternative reality, the world within the soul in whose quietude can be heard the mystic reverberations of infinity. Reality is not here, in the ceaseless conflict of the visible world, but elsewhere, in that 'sense sublime of something far more deeply interfused', the world of Platonic forms, or Pauline grace, or the mystic's rapture. This is not *Kohelet*'s conclusion, but it is an understandable one, and it has spoken to some of humanity's greatest minds.

Judaism's most revolutionary gesture is to have declined this consolation. At most times it has had its mystics and solitaries but they have not been, nor have they claimed to be, its representative voices. With unusual courage, often in dire circumstances, Jews have felt called on to bring the presence of God into the public places of our shared life. God is not in another world but in this, the world of deceit and desire, collision and collusion. He is here, less as a presence than as a challenge, a call, a summons, a command. It is not the world as it is that bears deepest witness to the existence of God, but the world as it ought to be, which is why creation is incomplete without revelation. We must resist the flight into solitude, for we are called on neither to forsake nor to accept the world but to change it, creating in its midst a society of justice and compassion, equity and moral integrity, never yielding to despair even after a succession of failures.

This cannot be a private task. Building a society is an essentially public undertaking. It needs the efforts of an entire people, sustained over many generations. That is why Abraham was chosen not because of his personal righteousness but 'so that he will direct his children and his household after him to keep the way of the Lord by doing what is right and just'. That is the basis of the event which brought the Jewish people into being as a holy nation: the covenant at Sinai. It was a covenant not with individuals in their solitariness but with a people in its collective entirety. For only a people can create a society, and only a society can bring God from the privacy of heaven to the public spaces of life on earth.

The Talmud says that when Moses ascended to heaven to receive the Torah the angels did not want it to be brought down to earth where inevitably at times it would be dishonoured. Moses challenged the angels. 'Are the Ten Commandments meant for heaven? Is there violence or passion or envy in the world of disembodied spirits, that they need to be taught that murder, adultery and robbery are forbidden?' The Torah is not meant for angels but for human beings in full recognition of their fallibility. Judaism is the sustained attempt to bring the Divine presence from the soul to the body, from poetry to prose, from the innermost mind to the public domain, from exalted moments into the texture of everyday life.

Despite its insistence on the dignity of the individual and the infinite value of a single human life, Judaism sees the person within a network of relationships, as part of a family, a community and a society. It is society as such that must be sanctified if the individual is to find God in the daily life of the world He created and pronounced good. The great symbol of Jewish spirituality is the tabernacle, a fragile sanctuary made by human hands and placed at the centre of the camp as a visible reminder that God is in the midst of the community as well as in the secret spaces of the soul.

Judaism is of its essence a collective endeavour, and as a result it is deeply communal in its spirituality. Its most sacred prayers cannot be said in private. The liturgy, other than occasional meditations, is written in the first person plural, not the singular. When we pray for an individual we include him or her amongst 'all others in Israel' who need healing or consolation. We confess our sins together. When a couple stand under the bridal canopy, the blessings said on the occasion, the *sheva berakhot*, speak of 'Zion rejoicing in her children' as if the whole Jewish people past and present joined in the celebration. Jewish mourning customs draw the bereaved gently back into the ambit of community at the very time when they feel most alone. Even the Jewish home is not a closed institution, a 'haven in a heartless world'. Jewish teachings emphasise the open house, the extended family, and welcoming the stranger. Hospitality is 'greater than welcoming the Divine presence'. We discover God in our togetherness, not our isolation. Martin Buber misdescribed the faith of Judaism when he spoke of I-and-Thou. The primary relationship in Judaism is We-and-Thou, the Jewish people standing collectively before God.

This explains the centrality in Judaism of the idea of law. Jewish tradition has many names for law: *Torah*, *edah*, *hok mishpat*, *din* and *halakhah*. What they have in common is the understanding that it is through our shared patterns of behaviour that God is revealed in the world. This idea has perplexed and occasionally exasperated those for whom spirituality belongs to the soul. Laws have their place, they would concede, but it is not in the realm of religion. Their role is limited and essentially secular, to preserve the social order and prevent people from harming one another. But if we believe that society can become a vehicle for the Divine presence, then law takes on a quite different character. It is the architecture of *kedushah*, the blueprint of a society that mirrors the goodness and order of creation. It is the arena in which we set aside our private inclinations and join our efforts to those of others in building a shared domain dedicated to God. Law is the expression of the We which takes priority over the I. It is the code not of individual salvation but of collective redemption, and this has implications for the concept of faith itself.

The Hebrew word *emunah* is usually translated as 'faith' or 'belief'. But like many words which lie at the centre of a unique way of life, it defies exact translation. When Abraham, old and childless, was told that he would have as many descendants as the stars of the sky, he 'believed in [*vehe'emin*] God', who 'counted it to him for righteousness'. This means less that Abraham believed he would have a child than that he trusted in God who had given His word. When Hosea describes God's relationship with Israel he says, 'I will betroth you to Me in faith [*be'emunah*]'. By this he means fidelity, loyalty, staying together in troubled times. *Emunah* conveys strength, firmness and tenacity. It characterises a moral relationship between persons, a mutuality of trust and dedication. As these two examples suggest, it is often a relationship created by words – a promise given, a betrothal spoken – and signals the power of language to express binding commitments. The key undertaking in Judaism is the covenant between God and the children of Israel at Mount Sinai. *Emunah*, in this context, means that both parties remain loyal to its terms.

Only against this background can we understand how faith, in Judaism, can be a communal phenomenon. The key concepts of Judaism – creation, revelation, redemption – do not refer to the relationship between God and an individual soul. They refer to the relationship between God and humanity, or God and an entire people. God creates the world not for lonely Adam but for people who marry and have children and build societies. It is Israel the people which experiences slavery and liberation; Israel the people which accepts the covenant and its commands; Israel which is charged in its collective life with being 'witnesses of God' and exemplars of righteousness. The prophet Ezekiel, in his vision of the valley of dry bones, sees the resurrection of the dead as something which happens to a nation, not simply to individuals. *Emunah*, as it resonates through the verses of the Hebrew Bible, is the faithfulness of a people to its shared and public undertaking. Individuals may sin, whole groups may break away, but the people as a whole endures and despite its many rebellions remains faithful to the terms of the covenant.

Believing therefore begins with belonging. We become Jews, not by formal declaration of articles of faith, but by being born into a people and accepting the terms of its history and constitution. That is why the sages of the Mishnah and Talmud, despite their exhaustive explorations of Torah, never formulated a definitive code of Jewish belief, and none appeared until the twelfth century when Maimonides wrote his 'Thirteen Principles' of faith. It was not because Judaism lacks beliefs, but because *emunah* means something other than individual assent to a set of propositions. It means identifying with a people, sharing its memories and aspirations, and participating in its collective encounter with God. Maimonides writes that one who 'separates himself from the community' forfeits his share in the world to come, and defines him as one who 'even if he does not commit any transgression, none the less separates himself from the congregation of Israel, does not fulfil commands together with them, is indifferent to their distress, does not share in their fasts, and goes on his own way as if he were a member of another nation, not theirs'. Nothing more powerfully expresses the participative nature of Jewish faith. I believe, because I belong to a people which has dedicated its collective life to God, and I have made their vocation my own.

Where then did belonging grow into believing? What was the schoolroom of Jewish faith, and which were its texts? They were the synagogue and the *siddur*, the book of Jewish prayer. We find traces of theological debate in the rabbinic literature, but the real battleground was elsewhere. It was in the liturgy that Judaism wrote its creed. Against dualism the morning service declared that God 'forms light and creates darkness, makes peace and creates all things'. Against the Sadducees who denied the resurrection of the dead, the second paragraph of the *Amidah* insisted that God 'restores to life'. The blessings over the Torah enunciated Jewish belief in revelation. The 'verses of praise' spoke of creation and the Divine presence in history. The rabbis discontinued an earlier practice of reciting the Ten Commandments as part of the daily service on the grounds that it was being used by sectarians to argue that only these, not the rest of Judaism, were Divine and therefore binding. They introduced a paragraph against schismatics ('For slanderers let there be no hope') into the *Amidah*, and legislated against leaders of prayer who used phrases suggestive of heresy.

In place of creeds, catechisms and articles of faith, Judaism had its prayers. The home of faith was the *bet knesset*, the place where the community gathered and rededicated itself to God. That is why the synagogue has held such a pivotal role in Jewish life, for it was there that Jews came together to identify with the totality of the Jewish people and its ancient but still lively covenant with God, committing themselves to continue it as the representatives, here and now, of the 'congregation of Israel' throughout time and space. By making the synagogue and its liturgy the guardians of faith, Judaism expressed the primacy of 'We believe' over 'I believe'. It was by being part of the 'congregation of Israel' and joining in its prayers that the individual participated in the journey, for some simple, for others complicated and full of hesitations, from fate to faith, from belonging to believing, from the member of an *am* to the participant in an *edah*.

There is a prayer we say every morning which, for me, perfectly expresses the Jewish experience of standing before God. It begins with a devastating confession of man's insignificance in the face of infinity:

> What are we?
> What is our life?
> What is our piety, our righteousness, our salvation?
> What is our strength, our might? . . .
> Are not all the mighty men as nothing before You,
> The men of renown as if they never existed,
> the wise as if devoid of knowledge,
> the intelligent as if without discernment?

As individuals we are nothing, a speck of dust on the face of time. And then comes a monumental 'but':

> But we are Your people,
> The children of Your covenant . . .

Collectively we are part of a remarkable heritage. We are members of the people who followed God into the desert, accepted His word at Sinai, built His home in Jerusalem, and stayed loyal across the centuries to a vision of 'the right and the good in the eyes of God', the building of a vast edifice of spirituality through the sanctification of small deeds. As the American writer Milton Himmelfarb once wrote, 'Every Jew knows how thoroughly ordinary he is; yet taken together, we seem caught up in things great and inexplicable . . . Big things seem to happen around us and to us.'

Jewish faith is learned and taught, lived and experienced, in community. That is why the integrity of the community, its inner cohesiveness and its loyalty to the founding terms of its existence, matter even more than the learning or piety of individuals. This is a theological proposition but its significance has not been lost on those who stood outside tradition. In 1955 Nathan Glazer, a secular American sociologist, expressed it well:

> The role that in Christianity is played by God's grace . . . is taken in Judaism by the holy community. It is that which touches and moves people, and brings them back to the faith. And the return to the faith, which in Christianity means the acceptance of beliefs . . . in Judaism means the return to the community, which is made holy because it lives under God's law . . . In Judaism, then, it is not God directly, found after an inner search, that changes man, but the example of the good and holy life, presented by the community of Jews.

Almost since its inception the United Synagogue has been criticised for the apparently strange phenomenon that 'as an institution it was orthodox, but it admitted to membership all who were Jewish according to orthodox criteria, irrespective of their own personal degree of religious commitment'. Many of its members were what is sometimes called 'non-observant Orthodox', and for this it was taken to task by both right and left. On the right, those who were used to the separatist

Orthodoxy of Germany and Eastern Europe wondered why a synagogue body should be open to and provide a spiritual home for those who did not live rigorously by its standards. On the left, those who were used to the secularism or religious liberalism that prevailed elsewhere wondered why the Jews of Britain should adhere in public to standards they did not necessarily keep in private. Why did they not simply form associations where what they did was declared to be the norm? The right accused it of latitudinarianism, the left of hypocrisy. Neither could understand what the United Synagogue represented.

The answer is that it represented something profoundly Jewish: the decision to be part of a community which embodies the Jewish faith of the generations. It was the classic gesture of *emunah*. Those who joined it were not necessarily strictly observant, nor did they thereby signal that they had through personal reflection arrived at all thirteen of Maimonides' principles of faith. But they were making a significant declaration none the less, that they wished to belong to a congregation which in its public and collective expressions remained loyal to the principles by which Jews had always lived, and whose faith they wished to see continued as a living possibility for those who came after them. It was not a personal profession of righteousness, but it was a decision to remain related to the community of faith. And it had significant consequences.

It meant that, whether frequently or intermittently, they were in touch with the Judaism of the ages, performing its deeds, sharing its prayers and aspiring to its ideals. It meant that they had not foreclosed the possibility of a deeper engagement with tradition, whether for themselves or for their children or grandchildren, for they had never institutionalised and thus perpetuated their private disagreements with it. It meant that they were open – and faith itself is a form of openness – to the voice of the Divine presence as it spoke through the texts and laws and prayers that the Jewish people had always held holy, and even if they did not hear it now they kept alive the possibility that they might one day. It meant that they were loyal – and *emunah* means loyalty – to the Judaism of all time, not just one time. The United Synagogue stayed open to them, and they stayed open to it. By drawing a distinction between the individual and the community, and protecting the latter against changes that might sever its connection with the 'congregation of Israel' extended through space and time, Anglo-Jewry was faithful to a fundamental of Judaism, that it is in community that faith must be kept alive.

10 · Community of Faith

At the heart of any institution is an idea. Marriage, parenthood, friendship, citizenship, each embody a certain way of life with its attendant obligations and expectations. There is nothing natural about institutions. They are the order we impose on the potential chaos of human relationships. At their best, they are complex works of art, continually rehearsed and re-enacted, through which we give living expression to some of humanity's highest moral and spiritual ideals. I want now to understand what idea lies at the core of the United Synagogue.

There was a time when all synagogues expressed essentially the same idea, that even in dispersion, wherever Jews gathered as a community and dedicated themselves to the service of God, the Divine presence was with them. It and they were in exile but they were not parted. The synagogue was both a memory and a hope, a memory of the Temple and a hope of future restoration, but between the two Jews could still live and pray and carry out their ancient role as a holy nation.

Under the impact of dramatic events, however, communities began to reflect on their experience and their relationship to the Jewish past, and not all of them came to the same conclusion. There were different kinds of Jewish community, each with its own sense of where it came from, where it was going to, and what its particular role was. Jews built their communities around synagogues – whenever they arrived in a new country their first collective request was for permission to build a house of worship – and it is in the names they gave their synagogues that we can best understand how they saw themselves. The name is daughter of the idea.

The first synagogue in America was called Shearith Israel, 'the remnant of Israel'. It is a name full of pathos. Its builders were Spanish and Portuguese Jews who had arrived in America through circuitous routes, but who were all members of families who had experienced the tragic events of the Spanish persecution and expulsion. Many of them had ancestors who had been forced to live as *marranos*, Jews-in-secret, and their families had spent the previous century and a half wandering in search of a place where they could practise their faith openly without fear of persecution. The name Shearith Israel speaks of a community which saw itself as the survivors of a catastrophe. They were the vestige, the faithful 'remnant' of which the prophets spoke, who would endure the sufferings of exile and eventually return to the land of Israel.

Two centuries later, when the Reform leader Isaac Mayer Wise moved to Cincinnati, an entirely different mood prevailed. Following the lead of the first Reform congregation, in Hamburg, he proposed to call his place of worship not a synagogue but a Temple. This was a deliberate revolution. In his dedicatory address in 1865 Wise explained that the traditional synagogue embodied a longing and a sense of loss for the Temple that had been destroyed and would one day be rebuilt. Jews in America, he argued, had no place for such sentiments. This was now their home and they wanted no other. They neither mourned the Temple nor sought to remember Jerusalem. Changing the name from synagogue to Temple was a deliberate rejection of traditional Jewish belief in exile and the return to Zion.

Yet another pattern began to emerge in the 1880s as East European immigrants arrived in their hundreds of thousands. Driven by a stronger sense of solidarity and ethnicity than the German Jews who preceded them, they created *hevrot*, 'fellowships', centred on the three classic principles of Jewish community: study, collective worship, and mutual welfare. Organised on the *Landsmannschaft* principle, they brought together immigrants from the same place of origin, and to emphasise this they were usually known as *Anshei*, 'Men of', followed by the name of the European town or region from which they came. Thousands of these *hevrot* grew up in New

York between 1880 and 1920, and they formed a rich network of meeting places and support groups through which the new arrivals could share memories of *di alte heym*, the old home, and create friendly societies which offered help in times of need – sickness, unemployment, marriage and burial. Their names signalled that they were communities of people from such-and-such a place, strangers in a new land, and that they would stay together, help each other, and recreate the life they knew elsewhere. The *hevrot* represented a religion-saturated ethnicity.

At the same time, other communities saw their role as combatants in an ideological war. Those who defined themselves primarily in terms of their opposition to Reform gave their congregations names such as *Machzikei Hadath* or *Shomrei Hadath*, 'Upholders' or 'Guardians of the Faith'. A letter written in the 1890s by the leaders of the London *Machzikei Hadath* congregation at the height of their controversy with Chief Rabbi Hermann Adler gives us a sense of their mood: 'We are therefore justly proud that this Holy idea came to us to take up the battle of the Lord of Hosts, so that the Faith of Israel shall not be forgotten by all.' Such communities saw themselves as lone guardians of Judaism in an age of assimilation and Reform.

The two most significant names, as we have already noted, were those associated with Samson Raphael Hirsch in Germany and Mordechai Kaplan in America. More than any other they illustrate the rift which developed in Jewry in the nineteenth century and which still divides it today. Hirsch's community, in common with other secessionist congregations, was known as *Adath Yisrael*. It was explicitly an *edah*, a congregation that had separated itself from the wider community or *kehillah*. As Hirsch himself wrote, 'Religious unity has not existed for some time and wherever it is missing, the enforced unity of the community . . . is nothing but an empty, meaningless form.'

Kaplan's decision – the polar opposite of Hirsch's – to call his Jewish centre a *Bet Am*, a 'house of the people', was perhaps the first time in Jewish history that a diaspora Jewish community had proposed organising itself on secular ethnic lines, with religious observance transmuted into 'folkways' serving no higher purpose than group survival for its own sake.

Each of these names bears witness to a period of intense and destabilising change. Jews had been exposed to social and political upheaval in an age of revolutions, and they were often its direct target. Caught between the twin forces of liberalisation and anti-Semitism, they faced pressures for which they were unprepared, and the synagogue became the arena in which dramas of adjustment and resistance were enacted. The names they bore signalled the paths their members wished to take. This is the context against which we must understand the significance of the name chosen by the founders of the United Synagogue. It was to be *Kehillah Kedoshah Knesset Yisrael*, the 'holy community of the congregation of Israel'.

There are many names for community in Judaism. In addition to the biblical terms *am*, 'people', *edah*, 'congregation', and *kahal* 'assembly', there is the rabbinic *tsibbur*, a legally constituted collectivity as opposed to an individual. When speaking of communal governance, the rabbis used the phrase *bnei ha-ir*, 'people of the city', or community council. In post-talmudic times the word *kehillah* was used to signify both an individual congregation and a larger regional assembly. But when the rabbis sought a term to describe the Jewish people as a whole, particularly when they wished to emphasise its character as a totality united across space and time, they used the phrase *Knesset Yisrael*, 'the congregation of Israel'.

The phrase is rabbinic, and does not appear in the Hebrew Bible. It occurs twenty-four times in the Babylonian Talmud, 248 times in aggadic midrash and thirty-one times in Rashi's commentary to *Tenakh*. It is not employed in legal contexts, but only in those passages where the sages charted the landscape of Jewish thought. It is the phrase in which they expressed the idea that the Jewish people is a mystical entity whose essential unity survives despite the fact that they appear to be no more than groups of individuals scattered across the globe. Specifically, it was the term they used to describe the Jewish people in its relationship with God.

> [During creation] the Sabbath day pleaded with the Holy One, blessed be He. 'All the other days have a partner, but I have no partner.' God replied, '*Knesset Yisrael* will be your partner'.
>
> 'I am black but comely' (Song of Songs 1:5). It was *Knesset Yisrael* who said this. 'I am black on account of my own deeds, but I am comely on account of the deeds of my ancestors'. 'I am black in my own sight but comely before my Creator.'
>
> *Knesset Yisrael* said to the Holy One, blessed be He, 'Even when You distress me, when You cause me pain, still You are my beloved.'
>
> 'Out of the depths I have called You, O Lord' (Psalm 130:1). The rabbis said that this verse was uttered by *Knesset Yisrael* who said, 'I am she and beloved am I. For though I am plunged into the depths of Gehinnom, when the Holy One, blessed be He, delivers me from its depths, I shall blossom forth in good deeds and sing a song before Him.'

In these and many other statements in a similar vein the sages gave voice to their deepest feelings about the Jewish people and the unbreakable bonds of love between it and God. Though they had sinned, they were not forsaken. Though they were in exile, the covenant remained. At times they came close to despair, but they knew that the Guardian of Israel neither slumbered nor slept and would honour His promise to redeem them at the end of days. *Knesset Yisrael* was more than the name of a people. It was the faith of a people, that their loyalty would awaken an answering response from Heaven. Though they had been driven from their land, they were not alone. In exile, the Divine presence was with them.

Above all, the phrase *Knesset Yisrael* signalled the rabbinic faith that despite their dispersion Jews were still one people. In the second century of the Common Era Rabbi Shimon bar Yochai taught that Israel was a nation 'like a single body with a single soul – when one sins all are punished, and when one is afflicted all feel pain'. His proof-text was the phrase in Jeremiah (50:17), 'Israel is a scattered sheep'. They are not a scattered flock but a scattered sheep, meaning that even in their dispersion they remain like a single individual. A remarkable talmudic homily states that just as Israel binds itself to God by wearing *tefillin*, so God as it were binds Himself to Israel. In Israel's *tefillin* is inscribed the unity of God. In God's *tefillin* is inscribed the unity of Israel: 'Who is like your people Israel, a nation one on earth?' (I Chronicles 17:21). 'The Holy One, blessed be He, says to Israel: Just as you have made me a single entity in the world, so I will make you a single entity in the world.'

This idea is so familiar that only with difficulty can we understand how remarkable it was. Prior to the destruction of the Second Temple no one doubted that Jews were a people. They were a nation in their land, and they were held together, as is every people, by bonds of politics, geography and history. Even when a section of the nation was sent into exile in Babylon, others remained in Israel and the exiles, sustained by the vision of the prophets, never lost hope of return. Within seventy years the hope was fulfilled. But by the second century of the Common Era, with Jerusalem in ruins and the Bar Kochba rebellion brutally suppressed, Jews had no realistic expectation of imminent return. The last days of the Second Temple produced no prophets of consolation, no Isaiah, Jeremiah, or Ezekiel, to keep hope alive. The most farsighted of them knew that Jews faced an unprecedented period of dispersion. There were already Jewish communities scattered across the world, but now or soon there would be no centre to hold them together. In what sense therefore were they still a people?

Imagine this, that at some time in the seventeenth century England had been conquered, its population transplanted across Europe, its main buildings and institutions destroyed, and the country and its capital renamed. For how long would English identity survive? For several generations, but not longer. There might be initial, abortive attempts at reconquest. There would be local gatherings of Englishmen abroad. They would share memories, think of old times, and keep the language alive. But their children or grandchildren would adjust to the new reality, learn the local language, adapt to the surrounding culture, dismiss their parents' longings as mere sentimentality, and Englishness would fade away. That was the prospect faced by Jews in the second century, and it allows us to understand the fateful significance of the idea of *Knesset Yisrael.*

It declared that Jews were still a people. They had none of the normal prerequisites of a people. They were not united by race or ethnic origin or geographical proximity or political association. They spoke different languages, had different customs, and dressed differently from one another. None the less they were still *Knesset Yisrael*, the Jewish people as a single entity before God. They were not merely a religion. Religions are not peoples. The Christian states of medieval Europe were a multiplicity of peoples and nations capable of waging war against one another. Religions unite individuals with God, not necessarily with one another. Jews constituted more than a religion, a set of 'churches', sects or denominations. They were a single cohesive unit bound by the covenant through which 'All Israel are responsible for one another'. Their dispersion was not the end of their collective life, because they still prayed and performed *mitzvot* and studied Torah, and when they did so they felt joined as in ancient times to God, the land of Israel and the totality of all Jews. Uniquely it was a peoplehood sustained by faith alone. Because they were an *edah* they were still an *am*. Because they were still a religious community – one community, not a collection of them – they were still a nation. As love and fidelity come together in the concept of marriage, so *am* and *edah* came together in the idea of *Knesset Yisrael*. It is not an exaggeration to say that without this idea the Jewish people would not have survived.

In it the sages re-asserted, in an age of crisis, the concept which drives the Torah itself, namely that it was the covenant at Sinai which turned Israel into a nation. It was neither the ethnic fact of common descent from Jacob, nor the political fact of sovereignty in a land, but the religious fact that all Israel had joined together to accept a constitution, the Torah, which would set God at the centre of their lives. The covenant included all Jews, men and women, young and old, pious and wayward, and all their future generations. It was not the code of an élite, of prophets or priests or princes. It was the text and context of an entire people.

Time and again the rabbis emphasised the inclusiveness of the covenant. 'Even the emptiest of Israel is as full of good deeds as a pomegranate is of seeds.' 'Whether they act as children of God or they do not so act, they are still called the children of God.' 'Any fast which does not include the transgressors of Israel is not a fast.' The 'four kinds' on the festival of Sukkot represent the four kinds of Jew – those with and without learning, with and without good deeds. Only when they are bound together do they secure atonement. 'Moses commanded us a Torah as the inheritance of the congregation of Jacob' (Deuteronomy 33:4) was interpreted to mean that Torah was the inheritance of all Israel, not merely of scholars. The crown of kingship may have belonged to David and his heirs, and the crown of priesthood to Aaron and his sons, but the crown of Torah was the inalienable right of every Jew.

The sages were familiar with the notion of a spiritual élite within Judaism. There had been the biblical priesthood. There were the pietist groupings in the late Second Temple period, *perushim* (separatists), and *haverim* (fellowships practising self-imposed ritual stringencies). There were sects outside the mainstream rabbinic tradition such as the Essenes and the Qumran sect known to us through the Dead Sea Scrolls. The rabbis themselves were a scholarly élite, sometimes at odds with the *am ha'aretz*, the unlearned. It is therefore all the more striking that the sages strove to avoid élitism, emphasising instead the solidarity and indivisibility of Israel. *Knesset Yisrael*, God's covenantal partner, was the community of all Jews past, present and future, united as they stood before God in their houses of study and prayer as they had once before stood at the foot of Mount Sinai. It was the concept of Jewry as a single community of faith.

This is the profound significance of the synagogue as a *bet knesset*. The key text here is the phrase, 'And I shall be sanctified in the midst of the children of Israel' (Leviticus 22:32). In its original context it meant what it said: God would be sanctified through the service of an entire people living in, or journeying to, its land. The oral tradition, however, took 'in the midst of' to mean ten people, a *minyan*, any public gathering of Jews for prayer. Rabbi Joseph Soloveitchik explains this quorum for public prayer in terms of the concept of *shelihut*, agency. Just as an agent acts on behalf of and represents the person who has empowered him, so whenever ten Jews assemble for holy purposes they represent not merely a congregation of worshippers but the Jewish people in its totality. They become 'the embodiment of the entire *Knesset Yisrael*':

> *Knesset Yisrael* is not just a collectivity, a crowd, a herd or a multitude. It is a separate entity, a living individuality. It embraces not only contemporary Jews but also the entire history of those people who have lived and died with *Shema Yisrael* on their lips. It includes the heroes and the cowards, the great and the small, the well-known historical figures as well as the anonymous people who are buried in unmarked graves. All are part of *Knesset Yisrael*. All are personified by ten ordinary Jews who gather together to pray as a *tsibbur* (congregation) . . . There is only one *Knesset Yisrael* and it prays with every *minyan* of ten.

The synagogue was therefore not merely what it had been in Ezekiel's day, an echo of Jerusalem. It was also the re-creation of the Jewish people. Those who gathered there were more than *a* congregation. In a halakhic and mystical sense they were *the* congregation, the re-embodiment here-and-now of the Jewish people as it had stood at Sinai and pledged itself to God. In the synagogue Jews anticipated not only the rebuilding of Jerusalem but also the physical and spiritual reunification of the Jewish nation. This is a deep and metaphysical idea, but it has been Judaism's genius to translate such ideas into living institutions, never more so than in the case of the synagogue.

It takes courage to assert an ancient idea in an age of crisis and make it live again in an entirely new environment. It marks the difference between renewal and mere clinging to the past. In the last days of the Second Temple, there were those who did indeed cling to the past. They were known as Sadducees. They were attached to the Temple, and within a generation of its destruction they had disappeared. The Pharisees laboured to understand not just the surface of Judaism but its subterranean traditions and principles, and because of this they and their heirs, the rabbis, were able to renew Judaism and rescue it from collapse.

Nathan Marcus Adler lived at another time of crisis. The structures of tradition were shaking throughout Europe and America. Whether it was the good fortune of conditions in England or the wisdom of his leadership, he made the decision to create in Britain a Jewish community that would resist the twin temptations of being Orthodox but exclusive, or inclusive but non-Orthodox, but would instead be faithful to one of Judaism's most majestic ideas, *Knesset Yisrael*, the community of all Jews standing before God. It took an unlikely combination of skills and circumstances for him to succeed, and naturally he did not do so completely. But he and Commonwealth Jewry did so more effectively than anywhere else, and their achievement has lasted for more than a hundred years.

It is sometimes believed that Anglo-Jewry made no original contribution to modern Jewish thought. It had no thinker of the stature of Hirsch or Rav Kook or Rabbi Soloveitchik. It produced no new synthesis, no ideology, no 'Modern Orthodoxy.' In a sense, this is true. Modern Orthodoxy is the name given to a self-conscious encounter between Jewish faith and modern thought. It arises when the need is felt to prove their compatibility. Anglo-Jewry felt no such need. Figures like Chief Rabbis Nathan Adler, Joseph Hertz and Lord Jakobovits were obviously at home in both Jewish scholarship and the wider culture of their day, and they won the argument by personal example rather than in the realm of theory.

But Anglo-Jewry did yield something new. Elsewhere I have called it Inclusive Orthodoxy. The difference is this. Modern Orthodoxy is concerned with ideas, Inclusivism with people. Modern Orthodoxy seeks to show that Jewish faith can be expressed in the language of contemporary thought. Inclusive Orthodoxy seeks to keep Jewish faith at the heart of the collective life of Jews. Modern Orthodoxy is about content, Inclusivism about constituency. Modern Orthodoxy, like Maimonides' *Guide for the Perplexed*, is an answer to the problems of an intellectual élite. Inclusivism is concerned with Jews as a whole, learned and unlearned alike. When Modern Orthodoxy succeeds it creates a philosophy. When Inclusivism succeeds, it creates a community. That is what Nathan Marcus Adler did, and it makes his contribution to modern Jewry no less significant than that of Hirsch.

I return to the question with which I began: what idea lies at the core of the United Synagogue? It is an idea quite different from that which governed most other congregations in modern times. It was a bold statement that even at a time when Jewish communities were fragmenting elsewhere, Anglo-Jewry would reaffirm the classic concept of Jewish religious peoplehood, *Knesset Yisrael*, the Jewish people as a single community of faith. This would require congregations to work together for the interests of the whole community. It would mean that they would on principle be open to all Jews, holding each of them to be precious whether they were observant or not, learned or not, committed or not. It would mean that Jewish leadership would have to be exercised in a way that was faithful and yet open, tolerant without ceasing to be firm. It meant that the United Synagogue could never rid itself of the tension between *am* and *edah*, peoplehood and faith, for that is what we are and in that endless wrestling match the congregation of Jacob has its destiny. It would never be as lucid as an ideological system. It would never be as pious as a separatist group. It would not be a community of saints or a gathering of scholars. But it would be what the Jewish people is called on to be wherever it is, *Knesset Yisrael*, the inclusive congregation joined by Torah to God.

That is not an insignificant task. That it was undertaken is impressive, that it was largely achieved, still more so. In an age of Jewish discontinuity, the idea of *Knesset Yisrael*, the community of faith, was somewhere kept alive.

Part Three
The Future of Faith

11 · Jewish Discontinuity

The United Synagogue came into being on 14 July 1870, and today the world to which it belonged seems almost impossibly remote. The term 'anti-Semitism' had not yet been coined. Neither had the word 'Zionism'. Ninety per cent of world Jewry lived in Europe. In Britain Queen Victoria was on the throne, the Empire was at its height, and it was said that 'To be born English is to draw first prize in the lottery of life.' Within Jewry the controversies of the first part of the century had subsided, and the mood was calm. In the summer of 1870 there were no intimations of the storms that were to break over Jewry and continue to break until the entire landscape of Jewish life had been transformed.

Little of what seemed secure then remains. In 1871 the first pogrom of modern times took place in Odessa. Ten years later they broke out simultaneously in more than a hundred Russian towns, sending millions of Jews into flight. By the mid-1890s Theodor Herzl was convinced that Europe was no longer safe for Jews. A half century later, three quarters of European Jewry had been murdered or burnt to ashes in perhaps the greatest tragedy of human, let alone Jewish, history. We still live in the shadow of that event.

Today Jews inhabit a world in which the State of Israel has come to birth and grown to maturity. The British Empire has disappeared. Two totalitarian leviathans, Nazi Germany and the Soviet Union, have risen, taken their terrible toll of human lives, and gone, and in the process, Jewry was shaken to its foundations. Its old home in Central and Eastern Europe – the synagogues, houses of study, yeshivot and Hasidic circles through which its inner life had flowed for centuries – was no more. Fragments remained, 'brands plucked from the fire', but nothing else. Where once nine Jews in ten lived, today there are fewer than one in five. Jewish life has moved from Europe to Israel and the United States.

For the last half century the great energies of Jewry have been spent on reconstituting itself as a people after the long night of destruction. Zionism was no longer a utopian dream. It was an urgent necessity. In Israel, in the land of their beginnings, Jews have begun life again as a sovereign independent power after a lapse of two thousand years, a phenomenon for which there is no parallel in human history. Less dramatically, but perhaps in the fullness of time no less significantly, the vestiges of East European Orthodoxy have been transplanted and begun to flower. Today in Israel and America yeshivot and Hasidic groups flourish unprecedentedly, the remarkable result of the work of a handful of survivors. The Jewish world has changed but it survives, and that, in this traumatic century, is no small miracle.

But today it confronts a problem which deeply affects the future of the Diaspora. If we were to identify a moment at which its dimensions became clear, it would be the publication of the 1990 National Jewish Population Survey in the United States, which showed that amongst young Jews, 57 per cent were marrying outside the faith. Intermarriage, which had stayed at low levels throughout the first half of the twentieth century, has since accelerated rapidly to the point where the very viability of American Jewry has begun to be called into question. Nor is the problem local to America. To a greater or lesser extent it is true of all diaspora communities in open, liberal societies. The challenge has been given a name: Jewish continuity. Like many new names it testifies to the sudden appearance of its opposite. What has emerged is Jewish *dis*continuity on a massive scale. Jews are ceasing to do what their parents and ancestors had done for millennia: create Jewish homes, have Jewish children, and continue the faith. The irony is overwhelming. Jews fought the battles of emancipation and Zionism for the right to be free to be Jews. Having won that fight, many are ceasing to be Jews.

Much has been written about Jewish continuity. I have

done so myself in my book, *Will We Have Jewish Grandchildren?* But the problem has not always been set in its full perspective. Intermarriage has long been a problem in the post-enlightenment Diaspora. There was a wave of it in late eighteenth-century Germany. In nineteenth-century Russia under intense anti-Jewish pressures as many as eighty thousand Jews may have converted to Christianity. In pre-World War Austria thousands of Jews annually declared themselves *konfessionslos*, 'without religion', as a means of separating themselves from the community. In the United States, on the three hundredth anniversary of Jewish settlement, an investigation revealed that only one of the twenty-three original families of 1654 still had Jewish members. Todd Endelman has told a similar story about long-established Anglo-Jewish families in his book, *Radical Assimilation in English Jewish History*.

Two things make the present concern with intermarriage different from the past. The first is its visibility. Previously, as older immigrant families disappeared their place was taken by new arrivals. The Sefardim in America and Britain were succeeded by Jews from Germany and Poland, and then by the large numbers who came between 1880 and 1914 from Eastern Europe. Jewish communities were growing. Though they were losing some of their more acculturated members, they were being reinvigorated by the influx from elsewhere. Western Jewry was being sustained by energies whose origins were far away. As long as this continued, there was little urgency to create local sources of Jewish inspiration. It takes foresight to see a spiritual crisis on the horizon several generations away, and communal will to act on it in time. Not until after the Second World War did American and British Jewry begin in earnest the task of building day schools and yeshivot. Today most diaspora communities know that they will not be replenished from elsewhere. If there is to be renewal it must come from within themselves. Such movements of Jewish population as there are, are primarily to Israel. Intermarriage therefore means decline.

The more significant difference is that it can no longer be explained by external forces. The Jews who left the community a century ago did so under considerable, if sometimes subtle, pressure. The corporate state of the Middle Ages was in the main content to let Jews be Jews. They were self-governing, self-sufficient, and formed an important sector of the economy. Jewish existence was often hazardous, but it rarely posed questions of identity. But the modern secular nation-state had no space for self-enclosed autonomous groups. It offered equal citizenship to all, but it demanded in return exclusive loyalty not only to the state but to its culture. Even in the United States, a nation composed of immigrants and dedicated to religious liberty, the strains of being different were considerable, and they were deeply felt by Jews. As John Dewey once remarked, 'For one man who thanks God that he is not as other men there are thousands to offer thanks that they are sufficiently like other men to escape attention.' Jean-Paul Sartre wrote perceptively about the Jewish passion for anonymity, for what he called 'humanity without race'. It lasted for two centuries, and with good reason. But it did incalculable harm to Jewish self-respect.

Few who left the community were as candid as Daniel Chwolson, a Russian archeologist in the nineteenth century who converted to Christianity. Asked whether his decision had been based on pragmatism or conviction, he replied, 'I accepted baptism entirely out of conviction – the conviction that it is better to be a professor in the Academy in St Petersburg than a teacher in the *heder* in Vilna.' But there can be no doubt that behind the many defections, conversions, mixed marriages and religious reforms of the nineteenth and early twentieth centuries lay a profound sense of Jewishness as a stigma in cultures still Christian though nominally secular. It is a palpable mood in all the writings of the period. No one put it more bluntly than Mordechai Kaplan in the opening sentence of his *Judaism as a Civilization*: 'Before the beginning of the nineteenth century all Jews regarded Judaism as a privilege; since then most Jews have come tc regard it as a burden.'

Today that has changed. There has been a profound transformation in the cultures of the West, partly as the result of the Holocaust itself. Societies have become self-consciously plural. Compared with a century ago there is immeasurably less pressure on minorities to conform. Jews are no longer the most conspicuous non-Christian group. In Britain they have been joined by Muslims, Sikhs, Hindus and others. These groups, together with a determination on the part of society as a whole to guard against racism and cultural hegemony, have brought a new variety to religious life and ethnic expression. Jews, especially those born since the 1960s, know that they are not outsiders. They have scaled the heights in every field: academia, the professions, business, politics and the arts. If anything, they are part of the establishment. Today, when the religious roots of western civilisation are spoken of, they are referred to not as the Christian, but the Judaeo-Christian heritage. There are no longer external causes for Jews to see Judaism as a burden, nor outside forces sufficient to explain assimilation.

Why then the sudden rise in intermarriage? There are obvious reasons, and I set them out in my earlier book. Young Jews marrying today are three generations removed from those who came to the West from Eastern Europe after the pogroms. Jewish identity can be sustained by habit and memory, but only for a limited period, generally for as long as we can remember grandparents who led a conspicuously Jewish life. The fourth generation has no such memories, and if it is to acquire a strong sense of identity it needs a powerful Jewish education. Jews survived the dislocations of the past because they invested in schools and made the transmission of tradition their highest priority. The ancient command of the *Shema*, 'You shall teach these things diligently to your children', was Judaism's central value and its guarantor of continuity. For a century, driven by the desire for social integration, Jews lost the habit of Talmud Torah. They neglected Jewish education while pursuing secular studies with a passion. The result was that by the fourth generation, as memory faded, there was nothing strong enough to take its place. Jews no longer knew why they should remain Jews.

That was the argument as I set it out two years ago, and I believe it to be true. But there is a deeper and more disturbing factor. It is that Jews have lost touch with faith.

When American sociologists began studying contemporary religious behaviour, they made an unusual discovery. They found that Jews ranked lower than almost any other group on the standard indices of religious belief. As long as forty years ago Will Herberg noticed that Jews were less likely than either Catholics or Protestants to say that they believed in God, or that they had recently attended a place of worship. In answer to the question, 'Is religion very important in your life?', 83 per cent of Catholics replied in the affirmative, 76 per cent of Protestants, but only 37 per cent of Jews; 88 per cent of Catholics saw the Bible as the revealed word of God, 85 per cent of Protestants, and 45 per cent of Jews. Of all religious groups in the United States in the mid-1950s, Jews were the furthest removed from the 'beliefs and attitudes usually associated with religion', and many studies conducted since have shown that they still are. In Britain, where patterns of religious behaviour are very different from those in America, a survey carried out for the Independent Television Commission in 1994 showed that Jews were less likely than either Christians or Muslims to describe themselves as 'very religious', to attend a place of worship at least once a week, or to say that religious beliefs affected their everyday life.

This is an astonishing fact and one that defies simple explanation. It cannot be because modern societies as a whole have become less religious. In fact, in the case of the United States, religious beliefs have held up surprisingly well, and the Jewish community is the exception rather than the rule. Nor can we attribute it to anti-Semitism or to the lure of assimilation, for they are far less powerful now than a century ago. It has been suggested that Jews have been the victims of their own success: higher educational and economic achievements are associated with lower levels of religious belief. Again, though, careful statistical analysis shows this not to be the case. The correlations are either non-existent or too small. In his *History of the Jews*, Paul Johnson hazards a larger speculation. Jews, he says, have always been iconoclasts and opponents of myth. Abraham broke his father's idols and the prophets waged war against paganism. In the modern world

Jews have simply gone one stage further and attacked their own beliefs. But though this may be true of estranged intellectuals, it can hardly apply to the majority of Jews, who attend synagogues, pray to God, and make sure that their children receive religious instruction, but do so with measurably less frequency and conviction than members of other faiths.

The loss of Jewish belief is one of the most unexpected phenomena in contemporary religious life. There are faiths which suffer an eclipse. Communism is one. In a generation from now, New Age mysticism will be another. But Judaism is not something which, like Jonah's gourd, grew up overnight and vanished in a day. It is a faith twice as old as Christianity, three times as old as Islam. No religion and no people has survived longer and in more arduous circumstances. Even its most impassioned critics saw in the persistence of Jewish faith something awe-inspiring and inexplicable. Luther was angry that Jews did not convert. Nietzsche was furious that they kept disturbing the conscience of mankind. Toynbee notoriously described Judaism – present so long after in theory it should have disappeared – as a fossil. But to each of them Jewish continuity was undeniable, even majestic.

Nor until the modern age did anyone have any doubt that Jews were a religious people. It was their faith for which they lived and at times were prepared to die. When they rose up against the Greek and Roman empires, it was in defence of religious principle. Throughout the Middle Ages, in Christian or Islamic lands, they resisted the threats and blandishments of absorption into the dominant culture. At all times they sought one thing – freedom to practise their sacred way of life. Even those who suffered conversion under the threat of death often practised their Judaism in secret and seized the first opportunity to move elsewhere where they could become Jews in public again. Whether they were admired or demonised, Jews were seen to be the bearers of an unusual, powerful faith. In one country after another, Moses' prophecy rang true: 'Then all the peoples of earth will see that you are called by the name of God.'

The debate about Jewish continuity has been frustrating

because of the deep reluctance of participants to see it for what it is: ultimately, a spiritual crisis. For more than a generation, Jewish life has been construed in primarily secular terms: ethnicity, anti-Semitism, Israel as a secular society and state, political activity, gifts to Jewish causes, Jewishness-as-culture rather than Judaism-as-faith. Where once at the heart of Jewish life there were synagogues, today there are fund-raising organisations. Jews have become an *am* while ceasing to be an *edah*. Under the impact of the Holocaust and anti-Zionism they have defined themselves as a community of fate, not of faith.

Not only religious leaders, but the most acute sociologists – figures like Will Herberg, Nathan Glazer and Charles Liebman – have understood that Diaspora Jewry cannot survive on such a base. There is no Jewish ethnicity, or rather, there are as many ethnicities as there are Jewish communities, each an amalgam of borrowings from the surrounding culture. Nor are they durable. The image of the *heym* which governed the lives of an immigrant generation, became for their children a handicap to be forgotten, and for the grand-children something to be recalled with nostalgia. But for the fourth, it is no longer there. As Arthur Hertzberg puts it: 'Ethnicity will no doubt last for several more generations, but it is well on the way to becoming memory. But a community cannot survive on what it remembers; it will persist only because of what it affirms and believes.'

Most importantly, ethnicity does not command. It tells me where I come from, but not what I should do or refrain from doing. It supplies me with no reason other than familiarity for preferring one way of life over another. Still less does it provide me with an obligation to ensure that my past should be my children's future. Only a faith commands. It alone speaks to me not only of memories but also of aspirations, in the case of Judaism perhaps the most profound a people has ever carried in its midst, to shape a society dedicated to the sanctity of life and the sanctification of daily living. The most salient comment in the continuity debate was made by Professor Barry Kosmin, director of the 1990 National Jewish Population Survey. He wrote: 'Organized American Judaism has largely failed to create a substantial body of true believers willing to sacrifice for their faith.'

Jewish continuity is to the 1990s what Zionism was to the 1890s. Both are central to the Jewish people and its survival in the modern world. The difference is that while Zionism addressed itself to hostility outside, continuity focuses on indifference within. Zionism was about the saving of Jewish lives. Continuity is about the saving of Jewish life. Zionism was about Jewry as an *am*. Continuity is about Jewry as an *edah*. A century ago Jews had faith but not a land. Today we have a land but we are beginning to lose the faith.

If *emunah* in Judaism were what faith is in other traditions there might be little we could do other than to wait for the culture of the age to change or for sudden illumination to light the souls of a new generation. The burden of my argument has been, however, that this is not the nature of *emunah*. Faith lives in communities where the great Judaic vision becomes tangible reality. Judaism does not ask us to wait passively for the experience of faith to strike. It asks us to join together, like the Israelites in the wilderness when they made the sanctuary, and create in our midst a space for God. 'We will do and we will hear' – Judaism is about the doing which leads to hearing the still small voice of God that whispers in the breath of life itself.

The single greatest challenge of continuity is to reverse the process initiated by Mordechai Kaplan whereby religion became ethnicity, the *edah* an *am*, the synagogue a secular Jewish centre, and Jewry itself a people that no longer worshipped God but group survival. What makes this still possible is the paradox noted by all observers of Jewry since the 1950s: Jews may no longer believe, but for the most part they wish to belong. Nathan Glazer called this the 'stubborn insistence on remaining a Jew, enhanced by no particularly ennobling idea of what that means'. By the 1990s this is beginning to fade, but while it exists so too does the possibility of continuity – if and only if the synagogue is at its heart. For it is in the synagogue that belonging becomes believing. In the *bet knesset* ethnicity is transformed into something altogether more spacious and inspiring. In it the

Jewish people is both *am* and *edah*. It becomes *Knesset Yisrael*, the Jewish people standing in the presence of God.

A traveller in Eastern Europe once found himself in the legendary town of Chelm. He was lost, and asked one of the locals the way to Minsk. The Chelmite contemplated the matter and replied, 'You want to go Minsk? I do not know the route, but this I know. You shouldn't start from here.' Renewing faith when so many Jews have lost touch with it is not simple. Given the choice, we would not start from here. But one fact deserves attention. Despite the epic changes since 1870, the United Synagogue still survives. So too does the model it created. Almost alone in Ashkenazi Jewry, the communities once influenced by Anglo-Jewry – Australia, South Africa, Canada, New Zealand and Britain itself – still preserve at their centre communities which embody the classic terms of Jewish faith. Their synagogues are predominantly Orthodox and their memberships are high. As individuals, Jews there may be no more observant than their counterparts elsewhere. But as communities they have made one decision which may yet prove fateful. They have remained loyal to *Knesset Yisrael.* They have not abandoned, modified or ethnicised Jewish life, nor is Orthodoxy confined to separatist enclaves. *Emunah* is guarded in the public domain where it must stay if renewal is to move not just individuals but the community as a whole. If we had to choose a place to start the journey to continuity, it would be here.

Anglo-Jewry is not what it was in 1870. It no longer stands at the forefront of Jewish life. It has neither the centrality of Israel nor the numbers of the United States. But the United Synagogue still dominates the landscape of our communal life. This is more than a historic achievement. It is a precious resource for the future. It means that we can still talk of Anglo-Jewry as a community of faith.

12 · Aspects of Renewal

There is only one way to renew an institution: to go back to first principles and ask why it exists.

The United Synagogue came into being to keep alive, at a time when other Jewries were fragmenting, the idea of *Knesset Yisrael*, the Jewish people as a single community of faith. It could never have hoped to attract all Jews, even all Ashkenazi Jews. A generation before it was born there were Reform congregations in England, and there were small Orthodox *hevrot* outside the mainstream. What it sought to do was to keep tradition and its standards at the heart of communal life, and to provide a spiritual home to which all Jews could belong.

Today many Jews are restless with this idea. The more committed would like to see it more exclusive. The less committed would like to see it more flexible in its interpretation of Jewish law and faith. In this respect the 1990s are like the 1890s, when Chief Rabbi Hermann Adler faced criticism from both right and left, the right in the form of East End Jewry, most notably the *Machzikei Hadath*, the left in the form of the Hampstead Synagogue which sought liturgical and other reforms. Now as then the United Synagogue must resist such claims, for they negate its very reason to be. It cannot move to the left without abandoning Jewish law, and it cannot move to the right without abandoning a large segment of the Jewish community. The United Synagogue is what it is because that, until the nineteenth century, was what all Jewish communities aspired to be, what indeed they must be if they are to be faithful to the mandate of *Knesset Yisrael*, the rabbinic vision of the total Jewish people in covenant with God.

The United Synagogue has not stood still, and has responded to the great changes in Jewry since its early days. Its services have become more informal. Wardens no longer wear striped trousers and black jackets, and rabbis have abandoned the clerical collar. New synagogues are less houses of worship than centres of community in all its forms. In Victorian England Jews went to the synagogue primarily to pray. Today they seek from it the full panoply of communal life: crèches, kindergartens, youth groups, social events, lectures, *shiurim*, singles' groups, women's groups and friendship circles. Congregations organise communal Shabbat lunches, *sedarim*, walks, visits, residential seminars and trips abroad. These are symptoms of a profound shift in expectation. In Victorian England Jews knew that they were Jews but wanted to prove that they were also unmistakably English. Today Jews know that they are English. They want to rediscover, in a more compelling and intensive way, what it is to be Jewish.

The religious leaders of Victorian Jewry would have been surprised at this transformation, but they would have welcomed it as a return to the classic role of the *bet knesset* as the centre of Jewish life in all its sweep and scope. They would have applauded the United Synagogue's investment in Jewish day schools and university chaplaincy. They would have welcomed the new dignity of the rabbi as a man of learning, and the sheer liveliness of the synagogue as a place of study. The United Synagogue has opened itself to a whole range of new influences, the yeshivah world, Hasidic rabbis, outreach groups, religious Zionism in its many forms and an old-new expression of women's spirituality. It is more diverse than it ever was, and so it more faithfully reflects *Knesset Yisrael* in its irreducible diversity. Old congregations in the centre of London, long dormant, have begun to thrive again. New communities in the suburbs burst at the seams. In the process some of the Victorian dignity has been lost, but in its place has come a new Jewish exuberance. Once Anglo-Jews were reluctant to dance in the synagogue on *Simhat Torah* for fear of earning the disapproval of men like Samuel Pepys. Today, bringing a new *Sefer Torah* to the synagogue, they dance in the street as King David did when he brought the ark to Jerusalem. Having passed the 'ordeal of civility' Jews now feel freer to be themselves.

In many respects the United Synagogue has never been healthier. Nevertheless, it faces a formidable challenge. Jews, like everyone else, have become internationalised, and the patterns of Jewish life in Israel and the United States have begun to appear here as well. Many young Jews have become secularised. For them Jewishness is a matter of ethnicity, belonging without believing. A minority has become more religiously committed, the *baalei teshuvah* or returnees who, since the 1960s, have in increasing numbers gone to yeshivah, re-engaged with tradition, and become more learned and observant than their parents. The former are unmoved by the synagogue. The latter want smaller and more intensive communities than the United Synagogue provides. Both represent a profound generational change between the classic terms of Anglo-Jewish life and the divided state of world Jewry today.

Synagogues alive to the challenge have responded in perhaps the only way they can. They have created multiple contexts of community: alternative services, explanatory services and *hashkamah* (early morning) *minyanim*. It is not unusual in some larger congregations to find as many as half-a-dozen services on a Shabbat morning, each for a different age- or interest-group. They organise social activities for particular ages, especially young singles. A group I started in a West End congregation a few years ago began with two people and grew rapidly to several hundred. These developments are not always welcomed, understandably so. A Jewish community ideally spans the generations and brings together singles, families, the elderly, the married, the divorced, those with children and those without, weaving out of their separate lives something genuinely collective. None the less, at this time of change and generational discontinuity it is almost certainly the best response. By addressing the spiritual and social needs of different groups within a single multi-faceted family of congregations the United Synagogue is faithful to its original task of maintaining an inclusive community of faith.

Perhaps the most profound change is that whereas in the past Jews came to the synagogue, today the synagogue must come to Jews. It must actively recruit members and devote considerable energy to the task. There was a period when the United Synagogue was endangered by its own success. For over a century it had been 'the establishment', one of the immovable pillars of Anglo-Jewish life. It took itself for granted, was capable of being bureaucratic and cold, and assumed that individuals would join out of habit because their parents had. It was just such a failure more than a century ago to reach out and respond to the new immigrants from Eastern Europe that led to the creation of the Federation of Synagogues, and it was one of Anglo-Jewry's great lost opportunities. Today rabbis and lay-leaders know that they inhabit a world in which, in almost every arena, habit has been replaced by choice in bewildering profusion. The synagogue cannot wait for Jews to find it. It must go out and find them, inviting them in and making them feel that they belong. This is difficult but necessary. Institutions renew themselves only when they can no longer take themselves for granted, and nothing is more likely to lead them back to their original sources of inspiration. In the case of the synagogue they are three.

In the *Ethics of the Fathers* Shimon ha-Tzaddik said, 'The world stands by virtue of three things, *Torah*, Jewish study, *avodah*, Jewish worship, and *gemilut hasadim*, acts of kindness.' Those who meditated most deeply on the role of the modern synagogue, Nathan Marcus Adler and Samson Raphael Hirsch, understood that these were the three-fold foundations of community. Adler did so in his first pastoral letter as Chief Rabbi, and Hirsch wrote along similar lines in an essay, 'The Character of the Jewish Community', shortly after his arrival in Frankfurt.

Significantly, the list begins with study, not prayer. Historically the synagogue began, whether in exilic Babylon or before, amongst Jews who gathered around the person of the prophet to hear him expound the word of God. Ever since, the reading and exposition of Torah has held a central place in the synagogue service. Torah study is the motor which drives Jewish life, and whenever communities neglect it they have already started on the route to decline. Hirsch was vehement on the point. He told his contemporaries, 'Yes, you should build houses of worship, establish philanthropic funds and artisans' guilds, but if you allow the Torah to remain unnoticed in a hidden corner, the spirit of idolatry will invade your houses of worship and all your charity will not be able to banish the spirit of misery, poverty and demoralisation from your midst.'

Torah – not simply 'that which is taught' but the process of learning and teaching, the ongoing conversation between parents and children, teachers and disciples – is the oxygen which Judaism breathes. An active community should have classes, lectures, *shiurim*, seminars and educational events of all kinds. One synagogue in London houses a full evening yeshivah. Some make a point of ending the Shabbat morning service early so as to provide an hour of study afterward for the whole congregation. Others have study groups every morning over breakfast after prayers. When I first became a rabbi I took it as my objective that as many people should attend study sessions during the week as came to the synagogue on Shabbat mornings, and we succeeded. Ideally every congregation or group of them should establish its own Jewish day school, and wherever there is already one in the vicinity it should be integrated with the community and its achievements celebrated as a matter of collective pride. The *heder* or part-time classes must never fall short of excellence, and education in all its forms – child, adult, family, introductory or advanced – must be the community's first priority.

Avodah, Jewish worship, is easier to define than prescribe. It is measured not by the magnificence of synagogue architecture, the virtuosity of the chazan or the presence or absence of a choir, but by whether or not it succeeds in making the congregation feel that it stands in the presence of God. *Kavanah*, spiritual directedness, is of the essence of prayer, and all else is a means to that end. When we pray we are not asking God to do our will but asking ourselves to do His. Using essentially the same words in which our ancestors have prayed for more than two thousand years, we merge our private concerns with those of the Jewish people of all generations, joining our voices with theirs in a choral symphony of praise and supplication. The aesthetics of the synagogue service change from age to age, but its purpose stays the same. It is to the soul, said Judah Halevi, what food is to the body. Without the experience of prayer, the spirit starves. Said three times a day, it cannot always be inspirational. The very word *avodah* means not only prayer but also 'labour', suggesting that spiritual uplift is never lastingly achieved without constant rehearsal. But *tefillah*, the act of Jewish prayer, is the supremely spiritual moment at which the community dedicates itself to the service of God in the presence of God, and at its highest we leave the synagogue personally transformed.

Gemilut hasadim signals the many social, charitable and welfare activities that must be at the heart of any Jewish community. The word *hesed* has been translated as 'covenantal love', and it means the relationship that holds between Jews as members of a single extended family. This is no idle metaphor. At one of the most solemn moments of the year, on the Shabbat before Tisha Be-Av, we read the blazing first chapter of the book of Isaiah in which the prophet rebukes those who attend the Temple but neglect the poor and powerless. Maimonides rules that we have not fulfilled our duty of rejoicing on festivals if we have neglected 'the stranger, the orphan or the widow' and failed to invite them to our celebrations. Today this means that a community must be sensitive to the needs of singles, the elderly, those living alone, the unemployed, those living on low incomes, the retired, the divorced or those experiencing marital conflict, the physically or mentally handicapped, and new arrivals in a neighbourhood. They must be valued and made to feel that they belong. Synagogues have always had pastoral and welfare concerns at their core. They were where charitable funds were collected and distributed and where provisions were made for those who needed practical or emotional support. The covenant which binds us to God binds us also to one another, and when help or comfort are needed they must be there.

These are the three bases of Jewish community life, and when they are strong it thrives. In this there is something more than good sense. There is deep religious insight, and to explain it I must say something more about *emunah*, Jewish faith. What philosophy was to Greek civilisation, *halakhah* – Jewish law – was and is to Jews. That is because, whereas for Plato truth was something to be discovered, meditated and known, in Judaism it is something to be lived. Moses, says the Talmud, gave 613 commands to Israel. David reduced them to eleven, Isaiah to six, Micah to three and Habakkuk to one: 'The righteous shall *live* by his faith.' *Emunah* is not faith contemplated but faith realised in life, by the way we live. The three great principles of Judaism are creation, revelation and redemption. That, I believe, is why the sages said 'The world depends on Torah study, worship and acts of kindness.'

In Torah study we live revelation. We listen to Torah as God's word, and through learning and teaching place it at the centre of our lives. In worship we live creation. In structure and style the Torah indicates that the Israelites' building of the sanctuary in the wilderness was the human counterpart of the Divine creation of the universe. As God made a space in whose midst man lived, so we are commanded to create a space in whose midst God lives. In acts of kindness we live redemption, building through small deeds a world slowly perfected under the sovereignty of God. That is why the synagogue is the home of *emunah*, for through our communal life the principles of faith become living realities for those who participate in it.

I visit many synagogues, and in the best of them faith palpably lives. In them we are caught up in something immeasurably vaster than ourselves and we participate in the great collective 'We' of *Knesset Yisrael* as it has journeyed through centuries and continents, betrothed to God. Judaism is supremely a religion of life. The Torah is a 'tree of life'. Moses tells the Israelites to 'Choose life'. In the laws of purity, contact with death defiles, for God's presence is in life. Most of the vast code of Jewish law is an infinitely detailed discipline in not taking life for granted, but making a blessing over it and sanctifying it. That is why, though Jewish communities can suffer a temporary eclipse, the Jewish people will survive, for despite the fact that its history has often been written in tears, it remains the most life-affirming of all religions, and has never been defeated by tragedy. To be a member of an outstanding synagogue, to be part of a community's celebrations and study and prayers, is to be glad to be alive and to be a Jew.

The renewal of our synagogues must hold centre stage in any plan for Jewish continuity. It is one thing to be momentarily inspired by an outreach seminar, a Jewish arts festival or a journey into Jewish history. It is something else to turn that inspiration into a lasting commitment that can be handed on across the generations. That requires participation in a community, one that is open, supportive and uplifting. That is the United Synagogue's greatest challenge. Much will depend on whether the most committed of the younger generation, those who have studied at yeshivot and spent significant time in Israel, turn inward or outward. If they turn inward, creating small congregations with limited contact with the rest of Jewry, they will have guaranteed the Jewish future of their families but they will have abandoned the community as a whole. If they turn outward, staying within the United Synagogue and exercising leadership and influence, they will change the lives of others and renew Anglo-Jewry. This in turn will depend on whether the central idea of the United Synagogue – *Knesset Yisrael* – still has the power to inspire. Speaking personally I think it does. In Judaism, faith lived is faith shared, and its home is in the centre of community.

13 · The Faith of a United Synagogue

There is no 'United Synagogue Judaism'. There is Judaism and there are Jews: one Judaism and an infinite variety of Jews. Indeed it is only the unity of the former that is capable of shaping a single people out of the latter. Without Judaism – one Judaism – there is only a multiplicity of groups, sects and ideologies which divide Jews and render them a set of subcommunities with less in common with one another with every passing year. That is why the United Synagogue has never formulated an ideology of its own. As a matter of principle it is open to the whole Torah, not just part of it, and to the whole Jewish people, not just part of it, and it refuses to compromise on either fundamental. It has sought to create not a philosophy but a community, a living community built on the principles of Torah and potentially inclusive of every Jew.

But the very process of maintaining an inclusive Torah community in a divisive age means that the United Synagogue has emphasised certain aspects of Judaism that are not always to the fore today, and these are worth spelling out.

Firstly it is a community of faith, loyal to the principles of Jewish belief as these have been articulated through the ages. This has not always been easy. Since the beginning of the twentieth century Chief Rabbis – especially Hermann Adler, Joseph Hertz and Israel Brodie – have come under pressure to admit more liberal doctrines, particularly in respect of *Torah min hashamayim*, 'Torah from heaven'. Hertz was eloquent in his refusal, saying to those who denied it:

> You have dethroned God; and you have put your own reason in His place. You pick and you choose among His precepts, retaining only those which suit your inclination or expediency. Though you play with words and still speak of divine Revelation, there is no longer a 'Thou shalt' or 'Thou shalt not', no longer a Moral Law that stands eternal and immovable in a fluctuating world of relativity. Man becomes the measure of all things, human and divine. We are back in the Iron Age of the Judges . . . There is no King in Israel; every man doeth that which is right in his own eyes.

Instinctively they knew – and everything in the biblical and rabbinic literature confirms it – that this was not *a* but *the* fundamental of Judaism. Alone among the peoples of the ancient world, Israel did not identify God with the sun or the rain or death or fertility, the great forces of nature. They understood that nature is often random, brutal and cruel. It has no moral purpose. Instead they discovered God in things not found in nature: righteousness and justice, moral responsibility and care for the weak and underprivileged. These values cannot be seen, they can only be heard; and therefore it is through words that God communicates with humanity. These words, contained in the Torah and forming the constitution of the covenant between Israel and God, are holy, which is to say something other than the words of man. For if the Torah were a merely human document it could be overridden by other human beings and we would have lost the greatest protection God has bestowed on mankind against our capacity, never more evident than in the present century, for error and ultimately evil.

The belief in revelation has come under massive assault in the past three centuries from several different directions. One, critical for Spinoza, was deism, the denial of a personal God who communicates with human beings. Another was the concept of history as evolution. Truth cannot have been revealed once and for all time, for human history is a form of progress from lower to higher forms. A third is secularism in one or other guise. The Torah must be a human document, the collective product of 'the Jewish people in search of God', since by definition all documents are human. Against these views, we believe that in Torah God has communicated His moral vision to humanity and His specific call to Israel. In it the Jewish people does not speak but is spoken to, by something greater than itself.

We are not fundamentalists, believing that the Torah is always to be understood literally, or that it yields its meanings without interpretation, or that faith demands the abandonment of intelligence. To the contrary, faith without reason is as tragic as reason without faith. In every generation there will be aspects of Torah out of harmony with the spirit of the age. In the early nineteenth century it was the return to Zion, which conflicted with the liberal Jewish understanding of citizenship in a European state. Precisely this example suggests that what one generation does not understand, the next generation may find the most inspirational of all. That is why *emunah*, faithfulness, requires humility, the willingness to stay open even to that which we do not yet understand, in the hope that one day we or our children will understand. The United Synagogue did not require faith from any of its members, knowing that for individuals it is achieved only after a long and perhaps never fully completed search. But it did preserve faithfulness to the great Judaic vision at the centre of its public life.

It is a community of *halakhah*, recognising the authority of Jewish law. *Halakhah* is Judaism's unique 'way' to God, turning abstract ideals into concrete acts and relationships, and making daily life a home for the Divine presence. A community of faith does not compromise the transcendent authority of *halakhah* by seeing it, as do liberal Jews, as subject to 'the autonomous self' (Eugene Borowitz) or 'communal consent' (Ismar Schorsch). To do so, as I showed in chapter seven, is to embark, however slowly, on the secularisation of Judaism, the path that leads from Solomon Schechter to Mordechai Kaplan and to an ever-widening breach with Jewish tradition. Jewish law has never been an expression of what Jews do, but of what we are called on to do, and it is as important to be able to hear the Divine 'No' as the Divine 'Yes'.

The United Synagogue has always adhered firmly to *hala-*

khah, permitting what can be permitted and forbidding what cannot be other than forbidden. It recognises that some of its members may not be personally observant, while others may practise greater stringencies than are required by the majority of authorities. It has striven to set a community standard, a framework faithful to Jewish law within which Jews, in all their diversity, can belong.

It is an inclusive community, welcoming every Jew, learned or otherwise, observant or otherwise, believing or otherwise, and seeing in each a valued member of Judaism's extended family. Few things are more central to what the United Synagogue is than this. Maimonides once wrote, 'It is not right to alienate, scorn and hate people who desecrate the Sabbath. It is our duty to befriend them and encourage them to fulfil the commandments. The rabbis regulate explicitly that when an evildoer who sinned by choice comes to the synagogue, he is to be welcomed, not insulted.' He was writing about Jews who had been forcibly converted to Islam, the *conversos* or as they were later called, the *marranos*. How much more so does this apply to those who publicly identify as Jews.

I have set out the foundations of inclusivism in my book, *One People?* Here I would only re-emphasise its centrality to the Judaic vision. It is the way of Abraham who, old and ailing, ran to bring strangers into his tent; of Hillel about whom the Talmud says, 'Shammai's impatience sought to drive us from the world but Hillel's gentleness brought us under the wings of the Divine presence'; of Maimonides who ruled that one should behave respectfully towards Karaites, drawing them close with 'bonds of love'; and of the late Rav Kook, Rabbi Soloveitchik and the Lubavitcher Rebbe, each of whom sought to bridge the gap between religious and non-religious Jews. As I put it in that earlier work, the inclusivist believes that 'Even if we must sometimes reject the beliefs and deeds of an individual Jew, none the less he or she is a fragment of the *Shekhinah*, the Divine presence which dwells in the midst of Jews wherever and whatever they are.' The sages pointed out the immense harm caused at various points in Jewish history when transgressors were driven away. 'Even if your left hand must sometimes repulse', they taught, 'your right hand should always invite back.'

It follows that it will also be a tolerant community, respectful of differences, defending its principles with reason and compassion, and seeking the best, not the worst, in all. This would not need saying, were it not that the Jewish world has tended at times to succumb to its opposite. We should therefore recall that the school of Hillel always taught the views of their opponents before their own. Ben Zoma defined wisdom as the ability to learn from all people. Maimonides told us to 'accept the truth from whichever source it comes'. The sages taught that, when the prophets criticised Israel they were rebuked by God. The Rebbe of Kotzk, explaining why Joshua, not Pinhas, was chosen as Moses' successor wrote that a zealot cannot be the leader of a community. One who follows the path of the sages, said Maimonides, may be humiliated but does not humiliate others; attacked, he does not reply in kind. His manner is gentle, he is the first to greet others, he speaks well of people, administers reprimands only when he knows they will be heeded, and seeks peace wherever possible. These are, or should be, communal norms.

It is a community of personal growth. In a passage which inspired the cover illustration of this book, I once defined it in the following terms: 'It is not the middle of the road. It is a moving escalator. The United Synagogue should not think in terms of static commitments. "He who does not increase his learning diminishes it", said Hillel. The United Synagogue's task is to move Jews from one level of commitment to another and higher level . . . Its theme should be *Shir Hamaalot*, a song of rising steps.' To be a Jew is by definition to be part of a journey, sometimes geographical, always spiritual, begun by Abraham and Sarah and not complete until the messianic age. To live is to grow, intellectually and emotionally, and the best way to do so is to be part of a community which continually poses challenges as well as offering the resources through which they can be met.

It is a community that recognises the centrality of the land and State of Israel. It prays for the welfare of the state, and observes the festivals of *Yom Ha-atzmaut* and *Yom Yerush-*

alayim, recognising in Israel's birth and Jerusalem's reunification events which call for religious celebration. Successive Chief Rabbis, in the prayers they have written for the state, have held back from describing it as *reishit tzemihat guelatenu*, 'the beginning of the flowering of our redemption'. Perhaps this was because they felt that, no longer having the gift of prophecy, we cannot say in advance whether Israel is or is not the beginning of a messianic fulfillment. Only in retrospect can we say what an event was the beginning of. But that is not to deny the central religious significance of what Israel already represents, the ingathering of exiles and the restoration of national Jewish sovereignty, two things for which we have prayed daily for almost two thousand years.

It is a community which is actively involved in the wider society and its culture. The first promise to Abraham, 'You shall be a blessing . . . and through you all the families of the earth shall be blessed', already emphasises the dual nature of the Jewish task, to be faithful to our own calling whilst being a blessing to others. Whenever free to do so, Jews have played a creative role in wider society, contributing to its economy, its professions, its sciences and arts. As Jeremiah told his contemporaries in the Diaspora, 'Seek the welfare of the city to which I have carried you into exile; pray to the Lord on its behalf, for in its prosperity you too will prosper.' Nor was this mere pragmatism. To be actively involved in the development of society is to contribute to the great Judaic vision of 'perfecting the world under the sovereignty of God'. To do so with integrity as a faithful Jew is to fulfil the command of *kiddush Hashem*, 'sanctifying God's name', by enhancing the respect in which Judaic values are held and leading others to say, in the biblical phrase, 'Surely this is a wise and understanding people'.

It is, in other words, not a segregated community. To be sure, Maimonides mentions that there are times ('like ours') when Jews may have to withdraw into their own enclaves: 'If there are evil men and sinners who do not let him live in the country unless he mingles with them and follows their evil customs, he shall go off to the caves, the briers or the desert, and not accustom himself to the way of sinners.' He was referring to ages such as his own when entire Jewish communities were faced with forcible conversion, the threat of which forced his family to leave Spain and go to Egypt. It does not apply to societies which practise religious freedom, and Maimonides' own role in Egypt, as physician to the local sultan and his court, is the proof. To be sure, in a society such as ours, whose values are often deeply at odds with the Judaic ethic, this requires that we intensify Jewish education and the institutions of Jewish life. But as Rashi points out in his Torah commentary, Moses told the spies that if they saw the inhabitants of Canaan living in fortified cities, behind walls, this was a sign that they were weak; if they lived in open cities, they were strong. It is a sign of strength that Jews engage with the wider world, contributing to its development, adding their voice to its ethical debates, helping to shape a larger society in accord with the universal laws of the Noahide covenant.

It is a community of communities, working together to do collectively what cannot be done alone. It is opposed in principle to communal separatism or secession. The sages interpreted the command, 'Do not cut yourselves' (Deuteronomy 14:1) to mean 'Do not split yourselves into factions'. Rabbi Naftali Zvi Berlin spoke about the fragmentation of the community into separatist congregations as a 'dagger in the heart of the nation'. It is often forgotten today that separatism only came to be regarded as a virtue in the twentieth century. In the nineteenth century, even those who fought for it did so as a last resort. Samson Raphael Hirsch, its most powerful advocate, stated explicitly that his action was the result of decades of provocation by the Reform-led community in Frankfurt, and that had he lived in Hamburg, where Reform was a minority, he would not have left the general community. In the *Machzikei Hadath* controversy which raised the issue of secession in Anglo-Jewry, the Hafetz Hayyim (Rabbi Israel Meir Hacohen) urged the congregation to make its peace with the Chief Rabbinate and the United Synagogue, as did Rav Kook who served as its rabbi in the years 1916–19. It is a source of great sadness that in many countries Torah communities dissipated their energies in fighting one another instead of working together to strengthen the community as a whole.

It is a community which accepts responsibilities to Jewry as a whole. The United Synagogue has supported facilities, among them the Chief Rabbinate, the London Beth Din, university chaplaincy, and hospital and prison visitation, which serve the whole of Anglo-Jewry. It has helped to inculcate the sense of *kehillah*, overarching community, which still characterises Anglo-Jewry at its best, and which is essential if it is to remain a single community of faith. It knows that there are many congregations not under its aegis and many Jews who do not share its principles, but it believes that 'all Israel are responsible for one another' and that a synagogue body cannot confine itself only to its own members. There is an old Jewish saying that the *hasidah*, the stork, is an unclean animal despite the fact that its name means 'the compassionate one' because it shows compassion only to its own kind. A responsible community plays its part in the welfare of all.

If I were to summarise these nine principles in a tenth it would be that the United Synagogue is, above all, an open community: open to the whole Torah, the whole Jewish people, and all sources of Jewish endeavour and passion. Just as there are open and closed personalities, so there are open and closed institutions. Those that are closed may be invulnerable, but they lack that conversation with otherness which is ultimately necessary to spiritual renewal and growth. There are times when institutions, like personalities, must insulate themselves in order to survive, but they are rare. Under the onslaught of secularism or aggressive reform, the defenders of Jewish tradition elsewhere chose this route, and emerged generations later intact and strong. It was Anglo-Jewry's good fortune that this was not necessary. Tradition survived in a position of leadership within the community as a whole, without having to retreat behind protective barriers. Today, as Jews are returning to more compelling forms of spirituality, the United Synagogue must not lose its openness, the result of a century and a quarter of wise decisions. Precisely because of it, it will find itself able to discover new, even unpredictable, sources of inspiration.

When the Israelites completed the sanctuary in the desert, Moses blessed them. According to tradition he said, 'May the Divine presence rest in the work of your hands.' That has always been the role of the synagogue, to bring the entire community together, old and young, rich and poor, righteous and not-yet-righteous, and create in their midst an openness filled by the *Shekhinah*. That defines the United Synagogue's challenge and its faith.

14 · A Personal Journey

The intellectual journey I have taken in this essay has been for me a personal one as well. I did not grow up in the United Synagogue and it was many years before I became convinced of its importance. In fact, the first time I was a regular participant of a United Synagogue, I had become its rabbi.

The first two years of my life were spent in an extended family. My grandparents on my mother's side lived not far from Stamford Hill, a centre of traditional Jewish life. The house was large, and we lived together with them and what I recall as a whole entourage of uncles and aunts, cousins and assorted visitors. My grandfather, an other-worldly figure always immersed in books, owned a little shul a few doors away, and it was there that I developed a taste that has never diminished for small houses of prayer, in which physical proximity seemed to create a mood of spiritual intimacy, a kind of closeness to God that made prayer seem natural and unforced. I loved especially the mournful tunes of the prayers, always in the minor key. Even as a young child I could sense the bitter-sweet quality of Jewish life in those melodies from Eastern Europe which spoke of places and experiences far away and mysterious.

We moved, when I was two, to the suburbs of north-west London. The nearest congregation was a United Synagogue, and my father duly took me along. I refused to go in. The building seemed too forbidding, the people too prosperous and self-preoccupied. This was not a *bet knesset* as I knew it. Shuls in my experience were small, and the people who went there were not affluent or acculturated. They were poor, usually immigrants, and they carried with them a burden of sadness. They were nothing like the people here. If this was the United Synagogue, I wanted nothing to do with it. Only many years later did I realise that it was just such a feeling that had led to the formation of the Federation of Synagogues in London's East End in the 1880s, on the part of working-class Jews who felt that the anglicised United Synagogue was not for them.

My father made enquiries and discovered that a mile or so further away there was a *shteibel*, a little synagogue in the house of a rabbi. Even for an adult it was a long walk, and for a young child something of a marathon. But I loved it. It had room for at most twenty or thirty worshippers. The rabbi was a silent, austere figure, but he instantly won me over by giving me sweets to eat during the service. Over the next twenty years I had occasion to pray in many synagogues, but they were all of this kind, small, unpretentious and without formality.

Once in a while I went to a United Synagogue, without finding spiritual satisfaction. The synagogues were too large, the atmosphere too anonymous, and the services less a participative activity than a performance in which the rabbi and chazan played the major roles and we, the congregation, were often reduced to spectators. No one welcomed us, we felt like outsiders, and we risked constant embarrassment by finding that we were sitting on someone else's seat. In short, I did not like the United Synagogue. Its synagogues were more like the Temple than the Tabernacle, and its services more like 'praying' than *davenning*. I felt that in its pursuit of Englishness it had lost some of the essential qualities of Jewish spirituality.

The change came in the course of the momentous weeks of May and June 1967. On 15 May, Gamal Abdel Nasser placed the Egyptian army on a state of maximum alert. Troops moved in force into Sinai. On 18 May, at his request, United Nations forces withdrew from the area. Four days later the Gulf of Aqaba was closed to Israeli shipping. War was imminent and its aim was the destruction of Israel. Conor Cruise O'Brien writes that 'the mood of the people of Israel came as near to despair as it had ever come'. It was a feeling that swept across the Jewish world. There were fears of a second Holocaust. I had begun my studies at university, and in Cambridge during those weeks of waiting the little synagogue was full of students who had not been there before, praying for a miracle. For many of us those days evoked feelings we did not know we had. As the Holocaust had been for a previous generation, so the Six Day War was to ours: the birth of the realisation that Jews are an *am*, a community of fate. As Shimon bar Yohai had said, 'When one is afflicted, all feel pain.'

The war came and ended, and there was exhilaration at its outcome. But for me it started a train of thought which has not yet ended, twenty-eight years later. What linked me to Jews I had never met, and with whom I had little in common, several thousand miles away? Whatever it was, it also linked me – I now realised – to the many Jews at Cambridge whom I had never seen at the student Jewish Society until then. I began to be aware how few of them, perhaps no more than one in five, identified with Jewish activities in the town. I was struck by the sheer numbers of my fellow Jewish students who were simply drifting away. If I was joined by a bond of fate with Jews in Israel, was I not also joined with them? It was a question that came back to haunt me over the next few years and was eventually to change the direction of my life.

What about the Jews who don't belong? The Judaism of the *shteibel* was ideal for those who went there. But what about those who did not? The *shteibel* was not an environment acutely conscious of the wider Jewish world. Where was the community that would connect those who were observant with those who were not, which was motivated by a sense of responsibility toward Jewry as a whole and which might address those who felt left out, excluded, uncomprehending, unwelcome and ill-at-ease? It was this that led me, slowly but inexorably, to the United Synagogue. For all its imperfections, it did care about the total community. It supported university chaplaincy, then in its infancy. It sustained the Chief Rabbinate, one of the few institutions to take a global view of Anglo-Jewry and its development. It did try to offer a spiritual home to the least and most observant alike. It strove to be both *edah* and *am*, an inclusive community of faith. Despite its occasional coldness, it took seriously the principle of responsibility, of being open to all and caring for all. It was the closest embodiment I could discover of the idea that had been so powerful at the time of the Six Day War, that Jews form a single extended family.

Eventually, after many detours, I entered the United Synagogue as a rabbi, and I was not disappointed. The communities I encountered were remarkable in their range and breadth. In few other places in the world would Jews so different in their background and levels of observance have gathered in a single congregation to pray together and relate to one another. The social and educational programmes we organised drew on an even wider circle, some to the right of the United Synagogue, others to the left. When, later, I became the rabbi of a congregation in the West End we would be joined by many tourists staying at hotels nearby. They came from a broad religious spectrum, from Hasidim to American Conservative and Reform Jews, and from across the world: Texans in cowboy boots, black Jews from Ethiopia, Indians, Russians, Scandinavians and Israelis in their dozens. I used to feel a thrill when we came to the line in the *Amidah*, 'And gather us together from the four corners of the world', realising that Judaism was still a great overarching canopy of faith under which Jews from different lands and cultures could find shelter together, a few moments earlier strangers to one another, but now participants in a single community. More than most other Orthodox bodies, the United Synagogue extended the boundaries of belonging.

Much in its future depends on quite practical questions. Will it succeed in revitalising its communities? Will it attract outstanding rabbis and be more concerned than in the past with their training? Will it recruit lay leadership with the vision and will to think about the young, and the long-term? Will it develop a serious strategy for Jewish education, as it had begun to do before financial pressures forced its curtailment? Will it develop a more outgoing personality and be more welcoming to those who find it aloof? Will it learn actively to recruit members instead of waiting for them to arrive? In many areas, the signs are that it will. A new generation of rabbis and lay leaders has brought an altogether more extrovert and innovative mood to what was once a staid organisation, and this is what the moment needs.

But much too will depend on the continuing power of an idea, that of *Knesset Yisrael* itself. Will Jews still be moved by the only idea capable of explaining our history and collective identity – that of the Jewish people as a single entity standing before God? Here the signs are much harder to read, especially as we survey the wider Jewish world. Israel, a secular state, has become an increasingly secular society. By the mid-1980s President Chaim Herzog had already warned of the growing rift between the detraditionalised majority and the religious minority. The peace process has intensified it to what sometimes seems like breaking-point. American Jewry, preoccupied with its own problems of continuity, has itself become aware of the sharp division between its strong and growing Orthodox community, some ten per cent of the total, and the remainder, beset by intermarriage and disaffiliation. Three years ago I published a book with the title, *One People?* Readers in America wrote to tell me that within their community the question was no longer alive. It was too late to speak of Jews as one people. The gap was already too wide to be bridged.

I have deliberately set this account of the United Synagogue against the backdrop of large ideas, because that is where its significance lies. Commonwealth Jewry is one of the last areas of the Ashkenazi world to preserve a tolerant, inclusive Orthodoxy willing to take a leadership role within the total Jewish environment. If it declines, something of great significance will be lost to Jewry as a whole. For this to be avoided, these communities must keep alive the value which has sustained them until now. It is possible that young Jews will no longer be moved by the concept of *Knesset Yisrael.* The more committed will make their way to small, independent congregations of the kind I grew up in as a child. The less committed will join liberal denominations or simply disaffiliate. If this happens Anglo-Jewry will replicate the developments that have caused such anguish elsewhere.

A writer on Jewish themes knows not to predict. Too much that was unpredictable has happened in our history, and doubtless will continue to do so. But he can say what is at stake. Jewry today faces a spiritual crisis. It has done so for some time.

Israel cannot continue on its present route of secularisation without deep internal problems. Those who built the land in the early part of the century had a strong series of visions. They were constructed around the themes of socialism, a return to the soil, and the kibbutz as the model of a new kind of society. They owed as much to Russia as to Israel, to Tolstoy as to Isaiah. But they were coherent and sustained a generation of pioneers.

Today Israel is fast on its way to becoming an affluent liberal democracy on the model of the West, and Soviet communism is no more. For the last few years the most thoughtful politicians in the West have spoken about the need to renew their own moral and spiritual traditions. They have asked whether liberal democracies can survive the breakdown of the family, community and moral consensus. What they ask today, Israel will ask tomorrow.

Israel has an unrivalled resource in facing these issues. It is called Judaism, perhaps the most powerful framework of family, community and morality that exists. Sadly, many Israeli children within the main educational system of the state know little about this tradition, and are either hostile or indifferent to it. The religious minority in Israel, meanwhile, is growing stronger and more extreme. The two groups have become increasingly confrontational in their relationships with one another, and the peace process has highlighted a profound conflict between religious and secular visions of Zion.

The proper context in which to understand contemporary Israel, as Ben-Gurion knew, is against the backdrop of ancient Jewish history. Israel is not the Diaspora. It is the resumption of a story that broke off nineteen hundred years ago with the Roman conquest of Jerusalem, the story of a people in its land. If there is one theme which dominates all others in the biblical literature it is that Israel's greatest danger is the loss of its cohesiveness and sense of purpose. An ancient drama of prophets against idolaters, and pietists against Hellenists, is being replayed between *haredim* and *hilonim*, religious and secular Israelis today. The old prophetic warning was that when Israel abandons its religious vocation a process is set in motion which damages the fabric of its society to the point where it becomes divided and weak. Were a prophet to step out of the pages of the Bible into the streets of Tel Aviv he would repeat the warning, and with reason. Though the prophets were imbued with the spirit of God they were also political realists, and that is what gave their message power.

A different scenario is being enacted in the Diaspora, but it is not unrelated. Having reconceptualised themselves as an ethnic group, Jews in America are discovering that ethnicity has little chance of survival in an individualistic culture unless it carries religious weight. That is why black Americans are turning towards Islam. In the long run, belonging is sustained only by believing, and many American Jews have lost touch with their beliefs.

For more than a century, Jewish attention was focused on the outside world. The problem was anti-Semitism and the task was physical survival. Today the peace process in Israel and the problem of Jewish continuity in the Diaspora have turned Jewish reflection inward, and we are troubled by what we see. Several generations ago a deep transformation took place in what one can only call the collective Jewish soul. Consciously or otherwise, many Jews stopped seeing themselves as 'a people loved by God' and began defining themselves as 'a people hated by gentiles'. The psychological cost has been immense, and we are beginning to be presented with the bill. There is no safe destination at the end of this road. Jews will learn to be at peace with the world only when they have first learned to be at peace with themselves. They will be at peace with themselves only when they have learned to make their peace with God.

One group has remained psychologically intact during these traumatic times: the most committed Orthodox Jews. Today, some within its ranks are in triumphalist mood. They know that, alone among diaspora Jews, they face no problem of continuity. Their identity is strong, their families secure, their education networks are burgeoning and their future is assured. The more thoughtful among them know, however, that triumphalism is utterly misplaced. No one who cares for the Jewish people can be content if his family is safe but others are not.

Orthodoxy holds a message for all Jews. But in many parts of the world it no longer speaks to other Jews. It exists behind protective walls in an antagonistic stance towards the wider Jewish community. This, as we have seen, was born in the 1870s in Hungarian and German Orthodox secession, and it has continued and deepened ever since. There are exceptions. Led by the late Lubavitcher Rebbe, first Hasidim and then the yeshivah community developed programmes of outreach to the unaffiliated. They changed lives and led to a generation of *baalei teshuvah*, religious returnees. But their effect was on individuals, not communities. The divisions which began in the nineteenth century have become institutionalised in the form of religious denominations which no longer speak a shared language with tradition. They must oppose Orthodoxy in order to exist. So whole communities embody closed, not open attitudes, and a continuity strategy based on a shared religious vision becomes difficult, perhaps impossible.

If we were to propose one thing which might begin to 'mend the Jewish world' it would surely be this: the creation of communities where Jews of all kinds could meet and encounter, in a reasoned, tolerant, inclusive way, the classic patterns of Jewish life and faith. They would not be instantly transformed. Some would continue to be non-observant, others would continue to be non-believing. But a series of possibilities would have been opened up. Jews would meet with Jews unlike themselves and learn to form a common life built on lasting relationships. The more learned might share their knowledge with others less knowledgeable. The more observant might become role models for other individuals and families. Jewish tradition might speak in accents less strident, addressed as it would be to a wider and more diverse constituency. Those who joined would have made a serious commitment, not a personal and temporary one only, but one that would affect their families over the years: a commitment to stay open and related to the Judaism that once united and sustained a scattered people over centuries of dispersion. Such communities need not be invented. They exist, and this essay has told how and why.

Most of us, in this uncertain age, have thought long and hard about Jewish identity. Since those days in the summer of 1967 I have tried to pursue such thoughts through whatever evidence was available to me: Jewish literature, history, and sociology. As a student, I made extended visits to Israel and America and in both places met with the leading exponents of Jewish thought. I can claim no authority for my conclusions other than that they have been tested and counter-tested as rigorously as I know how. Until the nineteenth century the Jewish people defined itself as a nation brought into existence by a covenant with God, an *am* which was an *edah* and an *edah* that was an *am*. Uniquely as a people, its very existence depended on a religious vocation: to bring God from heaven to earth in the form of a society that would be a home for the Divine presence. Not only they, but others, would sense that there was something unusual about Jews, their way of life, their persistence, their loyalty to an ideal through difficult times; in a word, their *emunah*. They would be, in a strange but unmistakable way, witnesses to the capacity of God's presence to change lives, even the life of an entire people.

Through the Torah and the teachings of the prophets Jews were the first to bring great truths into the vocabulary of mankind: the oneness of God, the sanctity of life, the priority of right over might, and the importance of freedom, justice and a striving for peace. Albert Einstein once said, 'The pursuit of knowledge for its own sake, an almost fanatical love of justice and the desire for personal independence – these are the features of the Jewish tradition which make me thank my stars that I belong to it,' and most Jews at most times have agreed. They staked their lives and the lives of their children on the proposition that they were the people of the covenant, moral heirs to those who stood at Sinai, observers of God's law, witnesses to His presence, in some mysterious but unmistakable way, participants in a vast drama of Providence and redemption. They did not negate the value of other faiths, nor did they close themselves off from other cultures. They taught that 'the righteous of the nations of the world have a share in the world to come' and they pronounced a blessing over gentile as well as Jewish scholars. But they knew that as Jews they had been born into a unique heritage of which they were the guardians. Unless it had inspired successive generations, Judaism would not have survived.

A secular state like any other, an ethnic group remarkable only for its lack of coherent identity – these are not values likely to inspire. And Jews – throughout their history small in number and always a minority, whether in a region like the Middle East or a country like Britain or the United States – have needed inspiration. Their strength, as the prophet Zechariah said, lay 'not in might nor in numbers but in My spirit'. That spirit now needs to be revived.

Jewish faith is not mysterious. It is born neither in private experiences nor abstract theologies but in institutions: the Jewish home, the Jewish school and above all the Jewish community, the place where we assemble as a microcosm of an entire people in the presence of God. In this story of Jewish identity, the United Synagogue holds an honourable place. It did so in the past. I pray that it does so long into the future.

The cover illustration by Beverley-Jane Stewart was commissioned to mark the 125th anniversary of the establishment of the United Synagogue in 1870 by act of Parliament. The theme is taken from Chief Rabbi Dr Sacks' words in his inaugural lecture as Jakobovits Professor of Modern Jewish Thought in 1989: 'let me propose one single image which defines the role of the United Synagogue . . . it is a moving escalator. . . . "Shir Hamaalot", a song of rising steps.' The picture shows the changing face of the synagogues over the years as representatives of the community from Victorian England to the present ascend from past to present. The Chief Rabbis of the United Synagogue are shown on the spine of the prayerbook design used to frame the picture.